THE 1ST-TIME B2B SAAS STARTUP FOUNDER'S COMPASS

99 COLLECTED PRACTICAL THOUGHTS ON
FUSING STRATEGY, PSYCHOLOGY AND TACTICS
FOR CLEAR-CUT SUCCESS

RICHMOND WONG

First Edition

Hardcover ISBN-13: 978-1-7381450-0-3

Paperback ISBN-13: 978-1-7381450-2-7

Electronic Version ISBN-13: 978-1-7381450-1-0

CONTENTS

INTRODUCTION

WHO THIS BOOK IS FOR

This book is for 1st-time startup founders in the B2B space. Maybe you're a software engineer, product manager, salesperson, doctor or lawyer building your first startup.

My bet is that although you're an expert at your technical skill, you yourself recognize that there's a lot to learn when it comes to building a product, marketing it to a specific audience and overall running a company.

HOW YOU WILL BENEFIT

The next chapters cover the gamut of getting Product-Market-Fit, marketing traction, sales optimization, pricing, churn reduction and general business advice I learned through the process of working with 150+ founders and senior decision makers at startups around the world.

These chapters are answers I've come up with to issues that come up again and again with the clients I work with.

The material in this book is also informed by my time working around the world (primarily North America and Asia) in several industries including B2B enterprise software, legal practice, coaching and journalism so you'll get a wider viewpoint than from authors who have only ever worked in one industry and/or in one market.

HOW THE CHAPTERS ARE ORGANIZED

These essays are arranged to take into account your attention span (alternating between technical deep dives and lighter fare) and topic variety while maintaining an overall narrative arc.

WHO ELSE THIS BOOK WILL BENEFIT

Those in the B2C space (founders, marketers and product managers) will also find value within these pages.

CHAPTER 1
HOW TO DIFFERENTIATE STRATEGY FROM TACTICS?

Use this 3-part framework to differentiate strategy from tactics:

🏆 Business Goal by 💡 Strategy → ⚙️ Tactics

Three examples:

🏆 Increase revenue by 20% by 💡 Expanding product line → ⚙️ Develop and launch 3 new online courses

🏆 Increase social media followers by 25% by 💡 Influencer marketing → ⚙️ Collaborating with 5 prominent influencers for sponsored content

🏆 Improve website conversion rate by 15% by 💡 Optimizing user experience → ⚙️ Simplifying the checkout process and improving site speed

CHAPTER 2
AN EASY WAY TO CHOOSE NEW BUYER SEGMENTS: THE WIDE-DEEP FRAMEWORK

"I've just been hired as Global Head of Marketing and I have no idea which buyer segments to pick!" she told me in a semi-panicked state.

From Toronto, I spoke to my client in Asia.

She had just been brought onboard by a healthcare software startup to expand into several new markets across Asia, North America and South America.

She didn't need to tell me she was scared - I could already tell from her eyes and tone of voice.

My client had worked in large corporates her entire career, with all the support and infrastructure that multinationals provided their employees.

So this was an unfamiliar experience for her. This was the first time she had been tasked with leading a Go-to-Market (not to mention, several at the same time) all by herself without backup.

"Relax," I said. "Let's make this decision-making easy for you by boiling it down to the fundamentals. There are two ways to pick your buyer segments: you can go wide or go deep."

PICK BUYER SEGMENTS BY GOING WIDE VERSUS GOING DEEP

Going deep is:

- Pursuing more customers within the current segment(s) you're selling to; and/or
- Increasing the frequency of their purchases; and/or
- Increasing their average transaction value

For example, think of Netflix converting more and more cable TV viewers to their service.

Or how Apple increased the Average Lifetime Value of its existing core customers by selling them new products such as iCloud, Apple Music and Apple TV+.

On the other hand, going wide is pursuing customer segments you are not yet selling to.

An example of going wide is Zoom. The company originally targeted the corporate market but expanded to also serve individuals and small businesses when covid skyrocketed demand for reliable and robust video conferencing services.

HOW TO DECIDE BETWEEN GOING WIDE VERSUS DEEP?

Go deep when you still have untapped opportunity in a customer segment.

Why?

Simple.

Because at a minimum, you've already developed:

- Marketing and sales messaging that resonates with that audience
- Customer relationships that you can turn into referrals
- Awareness of your brand in that market

In my client's case this meant going after more of the same (or similar) private medium-sized to large medical groups in her country because this particular segment still had plenty of untapped opportunities.

In sales parlance, there was plenty of white space to grow within the segment.

In many cases, it's easier to go deep than wide exactly because of the immediate 3 reasons above.

On the other hand, go wide when all your current customer segments are tapped out in terms of growth potential, or when you want to diversify your customer base.

In Singapore, compared to the number of private medium-sized to large medical clinics, there are only a handful of government-owned healthcare groups.

Most of the healthcare institutions within these government-owned groups are already using solutions so there are much fewer white space opportunities.

Rather than pursuing this particular customer segment that is potentially lucrative, but already saturated by well-entrenched competitors, my client would be better off going after different segments.

In her case, she decided to go wide by instead pursuing medical schools in Singapore.

Finally, can you go wide and deep at the same time?

Yes you can, assuming your team has the capacity and/or inclination to do so.

WHAT ABOUT THE SAME USER SEGMENTS BUT IN A DIFFERENT COUNTRY?

Since my client was responsible for expanding into several new markets within Asia Pacific and the Americas, would going after more of the same customer segments in overseas markets be considered going deep or wide?

I consider it going wide for these 2 main reasons:

- In most cases, you will be building up awareness of your brand from scratch (unless you're a global brand or a recognized regional brand from a nearby country)
- Marketing and sales messaging may need to be adjusted for the specific localized needs of your target audience even though it's the same general category of customer. For example, mid-sized law firms from common law systems vs mid-sized law firms from civil law systems have very different needs

Will you choose to go deep, or go wide?

CHAPTER 3
SIX WAYS TO PIVOT YOUR BUSINESS BY UPDATING PRODUCTS AND MARKETS YOU SELL TO

Is your business stuck? Here are 6 ways to pivot your business using real-life examples:

NEW MARKET + SAME PRODUCT

- **Arm & Hammer baking soda:** Repositioned the exact same product from a cooking ingredient to a versatile, natural cleaning agent and deodorizer

SAME MARKET + NEW PRODUCT

- **Nestle:** Added to its offerings in the coffee portfolio with the Nespresso machine and capsules, joining their existing Nescafe and Dolce Gusto coffee mixes

NEW MARKET + NEW PRODUCT

- **Facebook / Meta:** Bought VR hardware company Oculus in 2014 and has since introduced products such as the Quest 2, Quest Pro, Ray-Ban Stories smart glasses and Horizon Worlds

ENHANCE AN EXISTING PRODUCT + NEW MARKET

- **LEGO:** Enhanced the classic "analog" LEGO building blocks experience by adding in a programmable robotics component with the Mindstorms brand. One of Mindstorms' core markets are institutions offering STEM (Science, Technology, Engineering, and Mathematics) education.

BETTER PRODUCT (COMPETE ON THE SAME METRICS) + SAME MARKET

- **Apple iPhone:** On the hardware (not software) front, the iPhone has more or less competed year after year with other phone makers on the same broad metrics (CPU speed, camera quality, battery life and storage capacity)

DIFFERENTIATED PRODUCT (COMPETE ON DIFFERENT METRICS) + SAME MARKET

- **Bose:** Took the technology in their over-ear noise cancelling headphone (QuietComfort 35) and changed the metrics it was originally judged upon by adapting it to an earbud format with the QuietComfort Earbuds while staying in the same wireless noise-cancelling headphone market.

SUMMARY

Six ways to pivot your product and the markets to which you sell to:

1. New market + Same product
2. Same market + New product
3. New market + New product
4. Enhance existing product + New market
5. Better product (compete on the same metrics) + Same market
6. Differentiated product (compete on different metrics) + Same market

CHAPTER 4
A GUIDE TO CAPTURING YOUR TARGET MARKET'S ATTENTION WITH THE MARKETING QUADRANT

"What's the best way to get people interested in and buying our product? We don't even know where to find them."

This is a question I often get asked by early-stage startup founders I work with.

Here's the framework I use to help them make a decision:

1. At the highest level, all marketing is split into **online vs offline** and **paid vs free**
2. There are four possible combinations of the above (with examples):

   - **Online and Free:** Posting on LinkedIn, X/Twitter, Instagram. Also blogs, etc
   - **Online and Paid:** Buying paid ads on Google, YouTube, Facebook, etc
   - **Offline and Free:** Word-of-mouth, loyalty programs, partnerships
   - **Offline and Paid:** Snail mail (yes, this still works), industry events, billboards, transit ads, etc

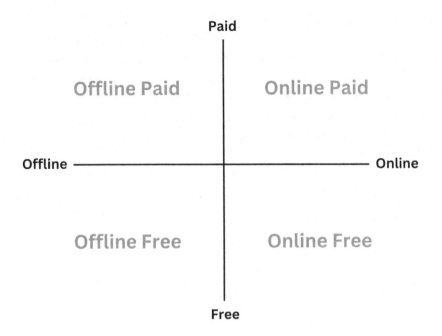

PICK ONE OR TWO OF THE FOUR METHODS FROM THE QUADRANT TO START

You want to focus on the mediums where your target market's decision makers spend their time. For example if you sell:

- Human resources management systems (HRMS) to early-stage B2C startups, then focus on free content marketing on LinkedIn paired with paid ads on LinkedIn or Instagram.
- Legal research software to the more conservative, insular and slower moving legal industry (say, mid-sized regional law firms), then focus on attending industry conferences and buying ads in the relevant industry trade publications.

ADD ADDITIONAL MARKETING METHODS TO THE QUADRANT AS YOU MASTER YOUR CURRENT METHODS

The ideal "end" situation is to have at least one method in each of the four quadrants. There are two reasons for this:

- **Diversification:** You spread risk across several marketing mediums. One of my mentors recalled the story of his client's $30 million health supplement business being destroyed when Amazon shut their account down. It was their only source of distribution. Bad idea.
- **Omnipresence:** Be in all of the same places where your target market's decision makers spend their time and attention.

CHAPTER 5
HOW DOES YOUR MIND MAKE DECISIONS? THE ANATOMY OF DECISION-MAKING

This formula is how your mind makes a decision for you:

📖 Information + 📊 Interpret + 🤔 Analyze

Here's how it works:

STEP 1: INFORMATION

Incoming raw information has 3 parts:

Quantity + Quality + Comprehensiveness

- **Quantity** = Total volume of incoming relevant data
- **Quality** = Accuracy and precision of relevant data
- **Comprehensiveness** = How many of the separate issues you're dealing with does the incoming data cover? For example, if you're dealing with 5 issues, does the data cover all 5 issues? Or just three?

STEP 2: INTERPRET

Interpret = How you initially perceive the raw data and the subsequent meaning you assign to it

This has 3 parts:

Domain Knowledge + Adjacent Domains + Relevant Non-Related Domains

- **Domain Knowledge** = Your existing topical knowledge relating to the raw data you're receiving
- **Adjacent Domains** = Knowledge that touches the borders of (or even overlaps with) your domain knowledge
- **Relevant Non-related Domains** = Non-adjacent areas of knowledge that you nevertheless are able to connect to the raw data based on your unique life or professional experiences

Your interpretations are shaped by how you see the world. And the way you see the world is shaped by what you know.

STEP 3: ANALYZE

Analyze = What you decide to do with the data you interpreted in Step 2

This has 2 parts:

Fluid Intelligence + Accumulated Knowledge

- **Fluid Intelligence** = Ability to solve novel problems without prior knowledge or experience with said problems. Also called "G-Factor" by scientists.
- **Accumulated Knowledge** = Domain Knowledge + Adjacent Domains + Relevant Non-Related Domains. Also called "Crystallized Intelligence" by scientists.

In this Analysis stage, you take the meaning from the Interpretation stage and make actual decisions with it.

And yes, the 3 parts of Accumulated Knowledge are the same 3 parts in the Interpret stage.

That's because you interpret and analyze with the same pool of knowledge you possess.

But what you DO with that same pool of knowledge is different in the two stages.

In the Interpret stage, you assign meaning.

In the Analyze stage, you make real-world decisions based on that meaning.

SUMMARY

Your mind makes all decisions by combining these 3 components:

$$Decision = \blacksquare\ Information + \blacksquare\ Interpret + \odot\ Analyze$$

Put another way:

$$Decision = \blacksquare\ Incoming\ data + \blacksquare\ What\ meaning\ you\ assign\ to\ the\ data + \odot\ What\ you\ decide\ to\ do\ in\ light\ of\ the\ meaning\ you\ gave\ it$$

In making any single decision, you may run through this 3-step loop multiple times.

More specifically, you will run through all 3 steps in your initial pass.

But subsequent passes may not involve any new incoming information and you will instead be toggling back and forth between interpretation and analysis.

CHAPTER 6
IS YOUR LANDING PAGE SPEAKING THE RIGHT LANGUAGE? HOW THE TERMS 'REVIEWS' VS 'TESTIMONIALS' SHAPE BUYER PERCEPTIONS

Should you call them "reviews" or "testimonials" on your landing page?

I personally prefer the term "reviews" over "testimonials".

Why?

Because the word "review" tends to be interpreted as being more objective - ie. reviews are *objective assessments* of your product, in which the providers of the review have the space to give both positive and not so positive perspectives.

On the other hand, the word "testimonial" gives much less of a sense that it is an objective evaluation, and that it is more of a commendation.

In other words, a testimonial self-edits out any negative aspects of the experience, however small.

In marketing, sales and persuasion, every single word shapes the frame of how you're perceived by prospects.

And the frame determines whether someone ultimately decides to buy or renew.

For many businesses, calling your testimonials "reviews" might be a more powerful way of using social proof.

CHAPTER 7
A TALE OF TURNAROUND: HOW CONGRUENT ADVERTISING TRANSFORMED AN AD AGENCY'S FORTUNES BY SHOWING, RATHER THAN JUST TELLING

You're leaving easy money on the table if you fail to show your prospects how you're Capable, Competent and Congruent for their needs.

Not too long ago I spoke to a business owner who was pulling low 5 figures in revenue each month but wanted more.

He sold "done-for-you" TikTok ad packages to small-scale gym owners and got his leads via Facebook ads.

I checked the copy of his Facebook ads and it was good. And the data supported this as just over 50% of prospects booked a discovery call after clicking the ad.

After that, about 40% of these prospects would become paid clients.

BUT THERE WAS STILL ROOM FOR IMPROVEMENT

And that was because he failed to show capability and competence that was congruent with his offer.

Huh?

You see, he ran static text and picture ads while trying to sell his target market on done-for-you video ads.

Wouldn't it be a far better idea to demonstrate his capability and competence in the first place by replacing the static picture with a video ad?

That would show his agency had the capability and competence to do so, in a format congruent with his offer.

- **Capability** = You can do it
- **Competence** = You can do it well
- **Congruent** = You can SHOW (rather than merely assert) you can do it

Capability is binary: either you can do it or not. Like a light switch that flips on or off.

Competence, on the other hand, is measured in degrees. Once you're capable, you're either more competent or less competent on a sliding scale.

And congruence? Well, it's showing indisputable proof you can do it.

Specifically, just because you possess the capability doesn't mean the prospect knows.

Even if you explicitly tell the prospect, that doesn't mean they'll believe you. At that point, they're still merely words.

YOU HAVE TO SHOW YOUR CAPABILITY AND COMPETENCE - AND THAT'S WHERE CONGRUENCE COMES IN

In the case of this agency owner I talked to, this meant replacing his static ad images with video.

In other words, communicating to his prospects in the same format that he proposed to help them grow.

Not only that, but creating a video that would:

- Grab a prospect's attention amongst all the other attention-grabbing clickable content on their Facebook feed
- Deliver a relevant and irresistible offer
- Feature on-camera testimonials from his existing clients for social proof and further demonstration of capability
- Finish by delivering a clear, direct and strong Call-to-Action

So what about you?

How much money are you leaving on the table by failing to show your prospects that you're Capable, Competent and Congruent for their needs?

CHAPTER 8
THE UNDERRATED VALUE OF LIFE PERSPECTIVE IN BUSINESS MENTORSHIP

Life perspective is just as important as expertise when finding business mentors.

Expertise is the "what-to-do" and "how-to-do" of the specific technical domain (copywriting, closing sales, managing remote teams, coding, etc) you're trying to get better at.

Perspective is what gives you the birds-eye view of the pros and cons of the what-to-do and how-to-do.

Personally, I look for another layer in perspective - and that's LIFE perspective.

In other words, how the actions I take (or propose to take) will affect (positively or negatively - and to what degree) my long-term effectiveness, health, relationships, wealth and contentment.

For this specific reason, most of my business mentors are far older than me - in their 50s, 60s and 70s.

While they've achieved great financial and material success, they also give me something that someone who has lived less of life does not necessarily have - and that's wisdom and life perspective earned from the ups-and-downs of integrating a busy business life with family, relationships, wealth-building and health.

Some of these guys wrecked their family life in the process of building their businesses, while others damaged their health.

Others tanked their net worth with poorly thought-out business decisions.

Most recovered, but all came away with a deepened perspective on living life and building a business.

Some were chastened even, but all of them always emerged with increased wisdom that would guide their later life - and to the benefit of everyone in their lives.

When seeking mentorship, who can you find who not only has the technical expertise to build your business, but can also situate the act of business building within the entirety of ALL your life areas so that you live a long, healthy, wealthy and satisfying life?

CHAPTER 9
ARE YOU MEETING YOUR PROSPECTS WHERE THEY ARE? UNPACKING THE 5 STAGES OF BUYER AWARENESS

Not all prospects are the same.

Some will need more time and education to move through your sales and marketing funnel before they buy.

Use the Five Stages of Awareness framework to:

- Meet your prospects at their current mind space
- Make them increasingly aware of available solutions
- Box out the competition
- Persuade them to pay you (rather than someone else)

Here's how you can use this model to get more prospects buying from you. We'll use the example of a new water purification device to illustrate:

STEP 1: PROBLEM UNAWARE

All prospects start here. In this stage, they have no idea they even have a problem - and thus they obviously have no idea about the different possible solutions on the market (including yours). The objective here is to make the prospect aware they have a problem that needs resolving.

Example: As a water purification firm, you need to educate prospects in this stage about the importance of clean drinking water. To do so, you may talk about the prevalence of water contamination or its harmful effects on health. The exact medium (social media, blogs, podcasts or paid ads) depends on where your prospects spend their attention and time.

STEP 2: PROBLEM AWARE

They now know they have a problem, but are still not yet aware that solutions exist (and what those solutions are).

Example: Here you introduce water purifiers (not necessarily yours) as a solution. To do so, you can use statistics and research studies on how water purifiers can make contaminated water drinkable. The objective is to establish the need for a water purifier.

STEP 3: SOLUTION AWARE

They're aware that there are different relevant solutions on the market that can resolve their problem.

Example: Water purifiers have been established in the mind of the prospect as a viable solution to contaminated water. Now you want to position YOUR product as the solution. To do so, emphasize (for example) the effectiveness of your purifier's filter, ease of use or longevity.

STEP 4: PRODUCT AWARE

Aware of your solution but they don't yet want it.

Example: They're aware of your product (as well as competing solutions) but they haven't decided to go with you yet. In this stage, you may want to use testimonials, compare your solution with alternatives to demonstrate superiority or offer a free trial to push them to your side over your competitors.

STEP 5: MOST AWARE

They've decided your solution has the necessary features that solves their problem in the way they desire. Now all you have to do is present them an acceptable price.

Example: The prospect is essentially ready to buy. You can push them over the edge with discounts, special offers or value-added bonuses (including warranties and after-sales servicing)

WRAP-UP

Keep in mind that not all prospects you encounter will start at the first (Problem Unaware) stage.

Some of them will already be further down the funnel (for eg. at the Problem Aware or Solution Aware stages) when you first encounter them.

In any case, your objective is to move your prospects through the different stages by making them aware of their problem, establishing your product as the ideal solution and then giving them the right incentives that make them buy.

CHAPTER 10
HERE'S HOW GENERALISTS CAN STAY RELEVANT ON THE MARKET

If you're a generalist, your highest and best use is as a unifier of the "little bit of everything" you know.

Maximize your highest and best use as a generalist by:

1. Using your understanding of the different moving parts within your domain(s) of expertise to…
2. …form a birds-eye view of how they all fit (and then work) together…
3. …with the intention to drive real-world actions that result in desired outcomes

Note that I am speaking of the above strictly in terms of the commercial marketplace where you are remunerated (in fiat money, payment-in-kind, crypto, etc).

If the area(s) where you are a generalist fall under your hobbies, then there is no strong necessity to have the ability to unify your relevant disparate skillsets. Go ahead, just enjoy it.

HOW GENERALISTS GET PAID

Being a hobbyist is fine, but if you want to get paid for it by creating commercial value in the marketplace (and thus maintaining your relevance as a commercial actor), then your highest and best use of your relevant generalist skills is to help clients (including your "internal clients" - ie. your co-workers) make decisions derived from the big picture understanding of your chosen domain.

Taking myself as an example as a Go-To-Market advisor, I am not a top 1% expert in either sales, marketing, product development, launch, risk management, operational efficiency or consulting.

However, I'm competent in all of these areas - but what's far more important is I can understand how all of these fit together (ie. how they are situated with each other, including sequencing) and their relationships with each other (ie. what processes/components flow between them and in what direction(s)).

From this big picture understanding, I am then able to recommend an action (or set of actions - including order of operations) to my clients to create the business outcomes they hope to achieve.

Now to be clear, this is something that works for ME personally, but it's something you may want to ponder if you are also a generalist.

CHAPTER 11
DON'T JUST TAKE COMMON "WISDOM" AT FACE VALUE BECAUSE YOU COULD BE MAKING LIFE OR LIFESTYLE THREATENING MISTAKES

"High risk, high reward"
"The pen is mightier than the sword."
"You can't have your cake and eat it too."
"Choose a lazy person to do a difficult job because a lazy person will find an easy way to do it."

Think carefully about what you hear and read, and don't by default take things you read or hear at face value.

Knowing this will prevent you from taking dumb, potentially life-threatening (or lifestyle-threatening) risks.

For example, taking "high risk, high reward" at face value by going skydiving with a company with known safety complaints made against it.

Or automatically assuming that laziness has a direct correlation to efficiency. Often, lazy people are just that: lazy.

Specifically, they're lazy people who don't accomplish much of anything.

Instead, be alert to your "Spidey-sense" telling you to look for the nuance (the grey) and don't think purely in black and white.

Life and business isn't binary, and much of it happens in the in-between. Therefore, your thinking shouldn't be binary either.

Accurate thinking matters if you want to successfully navigate the many complexities and nuances of life.

CHAPTER 12
"BUSINESS" IS FULFILLING PEOPLE'S DEEPEST WANTS

Some of our most powerful wants are to:

- Be liked
- Gain status
- Preserve status
- Gain control over others
- Be freed from responsibility
- Increase mating opportunities

Bestselling products combine two or more of these.

CHAPTER 13
IS YOUR MESSAGING RESONATING? FOCUS ON THESE 3 CORE MARKETING DIALS TO GET MORE LEADS

"We tried everything but we're still not getting enough leads - and the ones we do get, we can't turn into customers!"

When I hear clients say this, there's often something broken in at least one of these three core marketing dials:

1. Picking the right customers who want what you sell
2. Having an offer that is compelling to these buyers
3. Words, images and design that resonate with these buyers

Tweak these 3 dials and you'll have more leads, and more of these leads turning into customers:

PICK THE RIGHT CUSTOMERS WHO WANT WHAT YOU SELL

It all starts with finding the right buyers. In other words, people who have a current or anticipated problem your product can solve and/or who aspire to particular opportunities that you can fulfill.

The more urgent *and* burning these are for them, the more likely they'll act to resolve it.

But this alone isn't enough - and here's why.

The ideal customer segments are also those who have both the willingness *and* ability to pay.

For example, let's say that you help ambitious high school students who want to get into an Ivy League college ace their SAT.

While they have an urgent and burning aspiration to be fulfilled (as well as the willingness to pay) most high school students generally don't have the ability to pay (unless they have a job or freelance income).

Instead, your customer segment is actually their parents. They have a strong desire to help their kids succeed (and perhaps even earn personal bragging rights for sending them to Harvard), are willing to pay for it and - most importantly - have the ability to do so.

Make sure you're properly identifying the actual economic buyers (in this example, the parents) from those who influence the buying decision (their kids).

HAVE AN OFFER THAT IS COMPELLING TO THESE BUYERS

What makes a compelling offer?

At its core, it is one where the value (problems solved and/or benefits created) exceed the cost to the extent where it's an easy "yes" for the potential buyer.

A helpful way to think about cost is not the price ($99, $1000, $25,000, etc) the potential buyer has to pay.

Rather, it's the pain of staying stuck or regressing if they don't buy your solution.

Perceived and real value can be enhanced by value levers such as personalization, increased ease and speed of implementation, as well as support options (for eg. training webinars) and risk reversal (eg. money-back guarantee).

Not all value levers will resonate with your prospects. For example,

I've never cared about support options for any business software I've bought because I've always been able to figure them out myself.

The more value levers (that are relevant to your prospects) you can combine into your offer, the greater the perceived and real value your offer has for your prospects.

Finally, the greater the disparity between the stacked relevant value and the cost, the more likely your prospect will buy.

WORDS, IMAGES AND DESIGN THAT RESONATE WITH BUYERS

Finally, there's ad creative - basically the words, images and design of your marketing (whether it's online ads, Tweets, billboards, customer emails, etc).

There's a particular way I define each of these 3 terms:

- **Words:** Visual text (on your website, emails, social media posts) and your video / podcast scripts
- **Images:** Photos, illustrations and the visual portion of your videos
- **Design:** Split into UX and UI.
- **UX:** How you spatially organize your words and images on the page so that it minimizes any barriers to your prospects taking the action you want them to. For example, putting the Buy button in a place easily seen. Or making your website mobile responsive.
- **UI:** The visual aesthetics including color scheme, font choice, size of borders, etc. For podcasts and the audio portion (not to be confused with the script) of your videos, this would include soundtrack and sound effects.

The PASTOR framework is a helpful way to use words and images to maximize conversions:

- **Problem** = State the prospect's burning problem out loud
- **Amplify** = Twist the knife

- **Solution** = Tell them how you'll resolve the issue / get them what they want
- **Testimonials** = Show them proof you can do what you claim
- **Offer** = What you're selling
- **Response** = Ask them to buy or to take another desired action (for eg. give you their email in exchange for your lead magnet)

Then take the words and images you've organized in the PASTOR framework and incorporate it into your UI design such that the visual aesthetic and "vibe" match the traits or qualities your buyers identify with (for eg. rugged, dependable, future-focused, creative, etc)

SUMMARY

There are 3 fundamental dials in marketing:

1. Picking the right customers who want what you sell
2. Having an offer that is compelling to these buyers
3. Words, images and design that resonate with these buyers

It's important to identify buyers who need what you offer and can pay for it.

We've seen that a compelling offer isn't just about pricing, but about stacking enough value that outweighs the potential pain of staying put.

We've also looked at how to employ words, images, and design in ways that resonate with prospects, including use of the PASTOR framework.

Focus on these 3 dials and you'll have more leads, and more of these leads turning into customers.

CHAPTER 14
WHY WINNING IS THE BEST PERK YOU CAN OFFER YOUR STARTUP TEAM

As a startup leader, one of the best ways to build cohesiveness and loyalty amongst your team of ambitious colleagues is pretty simple: win.

If you're not yet winning, then demonstrate a trend towards winning.

Perks like generous vacation policies, catered lunches, half-days and pet-friendly offices are great.

But at the end of the day, ambitious people want to get ahead with their careers - and success in their current work is what they use to trade up to better opportunities (whether at your company or somewhere else).

IT'S ALSO NOT ENOUGH TO SIMPLY BE THE "NICE" OR "KIND" BOSS.

Yes, your staff still want to feel valued and listened to because they're human too.

But being in an environment where they're treated well, but consistently losing kind of...well, sucks.

At the end of the day, this personality-type wants to win.

And to do that, the entire team has to win - which means you as the team's leader need to make decisions (and take actions) that lead to wins.

At the very least, you need to show a path towards success.

After all, that's the main reason why they're here for the ride along with you.

It's not primarily because you're a "great person" or because you're "so understanding".

They're here to win with you so that they can win personally too.

So if they can't win with you, then they'll go find someone else they can win with.

Many ambitious performers don't see company-life as a family with unconditional acceptance.

For them, it's more like a sports team where performance is measured, taken into account for personnel-decisions and winning matters.

And there's nothing wrong with that.

CHAPTER 15
IS YOUR MINDSET HOLDING YOU BACK? CHANGE THIS TO CHANGE YOUR LIFE

What ultimately creates lasting change in us?

A mentor taught me this formula:

Beliefs = Thoughts = Actions = Outcomes

This means that our beliefs create our thoughts, which creates our actions, which results in our life outcomes.

Let's break each of them down:

- **Belief:** A conviction that you hold about something. This can be influenced by experiences or facts - or it can exist independent of these.
- **Thought:** This is what you say to yourself. Oftentimes, our thoughts are not verbalized to ourselves and are instead felt as impulses of emotion, or as a compulsion to take action
- **Action:** The actions (or non-actions) in the physical world that you take
- **Outcome:** How things turn out in your life as a result of the actions you take (or don't take). Your outcomes may also affect others as well

It may seem that the outcomes you get in life are created by your actions.

But a closer examination shows that it starts with your belief. The convictions you hold drive your thoughts, which translate into actions, which then ultimate create your life.

If you find that you can't change something about yourself (or that it doesn't stick in the long-term), it's likely because you're trying to effect change at the wrong level.

Instead, what you need to do is change at the deepest level - the level of your beliefs.

CHAPTER 16
A LOT OF LIFE ISN'T "FAIR" - BUT YOU DECIDE HOW IT ALL PLAYS OUT

Some are born rich, others are born smart while others are born strong.

Some are even born with it all.

But you work with the hand you're dealt and do your best.

No matter your starting point, you can still play your best hand by:

- Acknowledging what you're starting with
- Knowing that what you started with isn't what you're stuck with
- Amplifying your strengths
- Shoring up weaknesses in situations where having these weaknesses causes you problems
- Ignoring weaknesses that don't negatively affect you.

Life isn't fair and will never be fair - but you decide your next moves.

CHAPTER 17
IS LEANING INTO RESISTANCE THE KEY TO OVERCOMING PROCRASTINATION? A SELF-REFLECTION THAT MIGHT ALSO HELP YOU

I found that beating my procrastination is just leaning into the resistance.

I find that procrastination (at least when I experience it) has a lot to do with trying to get away from the mixture of different uncomfortable feelings I know I will feel if I complete a task in a way that falls short of the standard I envision.

This standard I envision for myself can be set at the beginning of the task, or it could fluctuate throughout the task.

Let me try to break it down and make things a bit more understandable:

If I'm writing something I'm invested in (such as this essay), that means at least one part of my mind will anticipate I will be judged by others (and myself) as stupid (or incompetent) if my final output falls short of the standards I imposed on myself (either when I started writing or during writing).

In short, a fear about being judged by others and myself in a way that is different (and negative) to how I currently see myself.

PROCRASTINATION HAPPENS WHEN AN IDENTITY WE VALUE GETS THREATENED

Basically, my identify at a fundamental level gets threatened. And my mind wants to prevent this from happening.

I therefore procrastinate because I'm unwilling to tolerate potentially experiencing the feelings that come from being judged by myself and others in a way that is incompatible with how I see myself.

And because I'm unwilling, in the first place, to tolerate experiencing uncomfortable feelings that threaten my identity, my mind purposely (but perhaps not consciously) avoids (or tries to avoid) doing certain tasks because it means having to first travel through these uncomfortable feelings before I can actually complete the task.

This itself comes from expectations I have for a minimum level of quality and/or measurable performance that I expect myself to meet.

Measurable performance includes:

- **Quantity:** A greater amount of tangible work produced overall (eg. writing 4 pages instead of 3)
- **Time:** Two possibilities here. First, a reduction of time spent on something (for eg. writing a blog post in 20 minutes instead of 40 minutes). Second, an increased amount of time committed to something (eg. Two hours of focused, deep work rather than 1 hour)

HOW TO LESSEN PROCRASTINATION

I've found that walking into the resistance (rather than the default of walking away) is what dissolves the resistance step by step.

Each step into the direction of the resistance (in this case, each word I type without overthinking or self-editing my thoughts) lessens the resistance more and more.

In this sense, each step into the resistance (even though it feels like walking towards something that will expose me as stupid or incompetent) increasingly quiets the assertions (ie. the verbalized and non-verbalized things our mind communicates to us) that cause me to equivocate.

And it is this equivocation that leads to doubt and uncertainty which ultimately manifests in my behavior as procrastination.

This essay isn't meant to offer a comprehensive or definitive solution to procrastination other than to suggest walking into the resistance even though we feel feelings of doubt.

The reason is that there are too many unknown unknowns around procrastination and I've not dived into any of the scientific literature or research around it to offer any sort of definitive or comprehensive answer.

ADDITIONAL NOTES ABOUT THIS ESSAY

- The operative word throughout this essay is MY procrastination. YOUR procrastination could be very different from how I experience and resolve mine
- I write to be "precise" about my procrastination, not "accurate". Accurate means how close I am to correctly elucidating what actually causes procrastination from a scientific/factual basis. I am instead aiming for precise, which means describing my own experience of procrastination in a way that matches as closely as possible (using the vocabulary known to me) what I experience in my mind. This means I try to describe what I experience - without regard about whether it is what actually causes procrastination from science's point of view.
- I am trying to capture all the small, interrelated moving parts of an amorphous, non-physical experience. Therefore, a lot of what I write may be quite difficult to read and come across as jumbled word salad.

CHAPTER 18
WHY I BELIEVE AUDIENCE SELECTION DESERVES MORE THAN 40% OF YOUR EFFORT

For the longest time, marketers swore by the 40/40/20 rule - that is, allocate 40% of effort each to picking the right audience and having an irresistible offer, and then the final 20% to ad creative.

I no longer think that's right.

After reviewing Brian Kurtz's book *Overdeliver: Build a Business for a Lifetime Playing the Long Game in Direct Response Marketing* for a second time, I've revised my view to 41/39/20 based on his advice and experience.

WHY LISTEN TO BRIAN KURTZ?

Kurtz is a former executive of direct response giant Boardroom Inc.

Over his thirty plus years there, worked directly with legendary copy-writers and marketers such as Eugene Schwartz, Gary Bencivenga and Dan Kennedy.

On top of that, he helped Boardroom generate hundreds of millions of dollars of revenue during his tenure.

So it's safe to say he knows a thing or two about running successful marketing campaigns.

Here are the specific reasons why I agree with Kurtz's view that the old 40/40/20 rule of thumb should instead be updated to 41/39/20:

PICK THE CORRECT AUDIENCE

Great ad creative (words, images, audio and video) and an irresistible offer is of no use if a completely wrong audience is selected.

For example, would you try to sell wisdom tooth extraction services to 5 year olds (or more precisely, trying to sell their parents)?

Or how about selling snow boots and winter coats to people living in tropical climates (say, Singapore)?

No, it makes no sense at all. And that's why I agree with Kurtz that correct audience selection is the number one priority (at 41%), rather than an equal peer of your offer.

HAVE AN IRRESISTIBLE OFFER

After picking the right audience, you need an offer that deeply resonates with them.

Great ad creative is the sizzle, but you for long-term success you still need a quality steak (your offer).

You might fool the market in the short-term using great ad creative to sell a shoddy product, but it inevitably catches up to you. Don't try to fool the market lest your business suffer the inevitable consequences.

COMMUNICATING VIA COMPELLING AD CREATIVE

No change here and this remains the third priority.

It's "only" 20% but this isn't meant to downplay the importance of compelling ad creative.

You still NEED good ad creative to be successful both in the short-term and long-term.

Rather, the 20 in the 41/39/20 rule of thumb is only meant to give you an idea of how to best divide up the pie when you start any marketing campaign.

Ignore any of these three parts at your own caution.

CHAPTER 19
CREATE YOUR PRICING STRUCTURE WITH THIS 3-STEP FRAMEWORK: PRICE POINT, BILLING FREQUENCY, AND FEATURE SET

Here's the 3-step framework I teach my clients to create their pricing:

Price Point + *Billing Frequency* + *Feature Set*

HERE'S HOW PRICE POINT, BILLING FREQUENCY AND FEATURE SET WORK

- **Price Point:** Do you charge, and if so, how much? For example, freemium, $49, $99, or $2999
- **Billing Frequency:** How often you bill. One-time lump sum for lifetime access? Recurring monthly? Every six months? Annually?
- **Feature Set:** What access users get. This includes the number of seats, API calls, functionality, speed, storage or support options. You're only limited by your imagination here

SHOWING HOW THIS WORKS USING A PRACTICAL EXAMPLE

Using a video conferencing product as an example, this might look like:

$79 + Monthly Billing + 1 user seat, 1 terabyte cloud storage, customer support via email / chatbot

HOW TO CREATE PRICIER OR CHEAPER PRICE TIERS

To create different tiers (Basic/Standard/Pro), you only need to adjust these 3 variables.

Using the same example above, an upgraded tier might look like:

$149 + Monthly Billing + 2 user seats, 3 terabytes total cloud storage, 24 hour phone support, transcription services

As you can see above, you can play around with the pricing structure itself to incentive longer-term contracts.

For example, offering a 10% discount if buyers buy a 6-month subscription upfront rather paying by month. And a 15% discount if they buy a full year.

Anyway, pricing is a place where you can get creative in maximizing Lifetime Value (LTV)...as long as you watch your numbers.

SUMMARY

- Pricing Structure = Price Point + Billing Frequency + Feature Set
- Price Point = What you charge
- Billing Frequency = How often you charge
- Feature Set = What the buyer gets
- Adjust any of these 3 to create more/less expensive tiers with appropriate levels of service and functionality
- Adjust any of these 3 variables to incentive greater Lifetime Value (LTV) from your buyer

CHAPTER 20
FIVE PRICING STRATEGIES TO INCREASE YOUR SALES AND SECURE STEADY REVENUE

Try these 5 ways to make it easier for your prospects and returning customers to say yes to your offers, and for them to say yes more often throughout the lifetime of your relationship with them.

In other words, these are 5 pricing strategies for more sales, predictable income and maximum lifetime value:

INCREASE CONTRACT LENGTH

Offer discounts to buyers willing to sign a longer contract. You can also up discount size as deal length increases.

Example:

- 1-year deal = no discount
- 2-year deal = 10% off
- 3-year deal = 12% off (+2%)
- 4-year deal = 17% off (+5%)

Advantages:

- A guaranteed, consistent revenue stream

- Increased customer lock-in as they integrate your solution over the long-term
- More chances to upsell and cross-sell throughout the life of the longer contract

TIERED PRICING

Offer different pricing tiers with varying levels of service.

Zoom's yearly plans:

- Basic: Free (max 40 mins + 100 ppl per meeting)
- Pro: $149 (max 30 hrs + 100 ppl + 5GB storage)
- Business Plus: $250 (300 ppl + 10GB storage + Translation)

Advantages:

- Capture more segments who would otherwise not be able to afford you
- Increase perceived value of more expensive options
- Price anchoring: In the Zoom example, the presence of the $250 plan makes the $149 option appear more affordable than if it did not exist

MODULAR PRICING

Allow customers to mix and match what goes into their product.

Tesla cars (any desired combinations of):

- Paint job
- Wheels
- Interior
- Steering
- Acceleration

- Enhanced autopilot

Advantages:

- Maximum agility in price adjustments. The ability to add or subtract individual modules allows for micro-adjustments in price
- Possibility to introduce complementary modules made by partner companies for revenue sharing
- Maximum agility in price adjustments. The ability to add or subtract individual modules allows for micro-adjustments in price
- Possibility to introduce complementary modules made by partner companies for revenue sharing

USER-BASED PRICING

Adjust pricing based on number of users.

Microsoft Office 365:

- Basic: $6.00 per user/mo
- Standard: $12.50 per user/mo
- Premium: $22.00 per user/mo

Advantages:

- Lower churn and higher usage per seat. As businesses are charged per user, they are motivated to actively promote product usage among their users, aiming to maximize their return on investment.
- Predictably scale pricing as user numbers increase

GIVE NON-MONETARY INCENTIVES

Instead of discounts, give incentives with high perceived value - but which are relatively inexpensive to you. It could be offering:

- Exclusive content
- Extended support
- Exclusive invitations to events
- Priority access to new features

Advantages:

- Increased perceived value that is difficult to quantify monetarily
- Strong differentiation. Buyers can no longer compare you feature by feature with competitors
- Strong emotional connection, loyalty & word-of-mouth if the incentives are seen as rare & valuable

SUMMARY

For more sales, predictable income and maximum lifetime value (LTV) try one or more of these (you can also combine them):

1. Increasing contract length
2. Tiered pricing
3. Modular pricing
4. User-based pricing
5. Giving non-monetary incentives

CHAPTER 21
HOW TO FINE-TUNE YOUR PRICE POINT USING VALUE-BASED PRICING

The three starting points for picking a price point are: competition, cost of production and value.

1. **Competition:** You pretty much follow the pricing of your direct competitors. Often used for commodities where there is little to no differentiation between your product and theirs (eg. coal, apples, cotton). You can differentiate via positioning (eg. Sunkist-branded oranges vs "regular" oranges), but a bit too complicated for this post.

2. **Cost of Production:** You come up with a price point price around what it cost you to make your product. You can price below (eg. as a loss-leader) or above, but you begin with Cost of Goods (COGS) as an initial starting point and price relatively tightly around it.

3. **Value-based:** Price point which your buyer is willing to pay, based solely on the end value your product will deliver to them. The highest leverage form of picking a Price Point and often used for software and information products. For example, if I wrote a little 3-page pamphlet that taught you how to make $2 million within 30 days guaranteed, I bet you would easily pay me $50,000 for it - even if the booklet took me just 30 minutes to write. Another form of value-based pricing

is charging by percentage of improvement: pay me 10% of every $1,000,000 I make you.

PICK VALUE-BASED PRICING AND HOW TO MAXIMIZE WHAT YOU CAN CHARGE

When I work with clients, I like to use value-based pricing with their offer given that there's theoretically no ceiling to it (generally speaking).

The general rule of thumb is: the more value (that is RELEVANT to your buyer) you can bundle together, the more you can charge.

The way to do this is via offer stacking - piling on as much value as possible and charging accordingly for different levels of value, functionality and support offered by your different price point tiers (eg. Basic vs Pro vs Premium).

The next step is to look at what competitors are charging, and to benchmark the relevant value of your offer against theirs.

The question to ask is: could you charge more given the relevant value you're offering (and promise to deliver on)?

If the answer is yes, then you can charge more. If not, then charge less.

Again, the key thing to keep in mind is: stacking value that is RELE-VANT to your would-be buyer. If you were a dentist, you would not pitch toddler wisdom teeth extraction services to parents (the economic buyers) with preschool-aged kids.

And remember, when we talk about relevant value, it means as it is judged by your would-be buyer (and not what you think is relevant to them).

CHAPTER 22
FINE-TUNING YOUR SALES USING SOCIAL PROOF: THE RELEVANCE AND AUTHORITY FRAMEWORK

Not all social proof (reviews, testimonials, case studies, customer logos, etc) are created equal.

This results in failed conversions and lost repeat sales.

HOW TO FIX THE PROBLEM OF INEFFECTIVE SOCIAL PROOF CAUSING FAILED CONVERSIONS AND LOST REPEAT SALES

Here's 2 things in your social proof you need to get right:

- Relevance signals
- Authority signals

One of the biggest reasons prospects and customers disengage from you during the sales process despite all the social proof you throw at them is because they lack sufficient Relevance and Authority.

In other words, it's not as simple as throwing any random testimonial, case study or logo on your landing page.

Instead, Relevance and Authority supercharge social proof to validate the following 3 types of choices for prospects/customers.

These 3 types of choices are those they:

- Have already made
- Currently are in the process of making
- Hope to make

Why? Because validating with Relevant and Authoritative social proof means the following:

- Validating past choices = gets them to buy again
- Validating current and upcoming choices = accelerates the buying process AND increases the chances they will choose you over competitors

Relevancy and Authority not only amplify social proof's power, but also determine its overall effectiveness.

- **Relevance:** Do your case studies, testimonials and logos precisely answer the following 2 relevancy questions. First, can you can solve your prospect/buyer's pain points? Second, can you can create desired benefits for them?
- **Authority:** Do the people or companies behind the testimonials, case studies or logos have sufficient credibility and standing with your prospect/buyer?

THREE EXAMPLES OF VARYING DEGREES OF RELEVANCE AND AUTHORITY IN ACTION

- **Example 1 (JUST Relevance):** If you're selling billing software to global law firms, using a testimonial from an entry-level billing coordinator at a top-10 firm saying how much time your product saved compared to their prior solution.

In the above example, there's relevance (a peer or near-peer organization in the same industry), but not enough authority (testimonial from a junior)

- **Example 2 (JUST Authority):** If you're selling cloud storage to small software development agencies, using logos from McKinsey, Goldman Sachs and Morgan Stanley.

In this example, there's authority (all elite firms) but no relevance (completely different industries and organizational sizes)

Instead, you need both relevance and authority:

- **Example 3 (BOTH Relevance + Authority):** A testimonial from a law firm senior partner from a top-10 firm saying how your product helped them increase cash flow because you made it much easier to track and collect accounts receivable.

See how this works?

And if we were to rework the cloud storage example from Example 2, we can achieve both relevance and authority by using logos from similarly-sized peer, near-peer or more elite software development agencies serving the same client niche.

SUMMARY

- Lost sales and failed conversions happen despite all the social proof (case studies, testimonials, logos) companies throw at them because prospects don't feel certain
- To solve this, make sure prospects and customers feel certain by validating (using social proof with Relevance and Authority) their past choices, and current + upcoming choices.
- Validating past choices = gets them to buy again
- Validating current and upcoming choices = accelerates the buying process and increases the chances they will choose you over competitors

CHAPTER 23
HOW TO BE YOUR CUSTOMER'S INDISPENSABLE PARTNER

Turn yourself from a mere seller of products into an indispensable partner by helping people achieve the material, emotional, health or relationship aspirations that give them hope amongst their daily life of rules and routines.

CHAPTER 24
MAKING THE TRANSITION FROM EMPLOYEE TO ENTREPRENEUR: WHY YOUR EXPERTISE AS A SPECIALIST COULD BE YOUR DOWNFALL

If you're just starting your first company, it's likely that your biggest strength as an employee is also your biggest weakness as an entrepreneur.

As an employee, what makes you valuable to your employer is your skill as a functional expert, often in one (or at most two) narrow areas.

The in-house lawyer drafts and reviews contracts but can't sell (or feels it's beneath them).

The salesperson finds and closes individual prospects but has no idea how to market online at scale.

The engineer can write code but has no idea how to identify profitable market niches.

SO WHAT'S THE PROBLEM IF I'M GOOD AT MY CORE AREA OF EXPERTISE?

The common problem in the examples above is that most employees only really have strong familiarity (or competence) in their tiny role within the machinery of business - this means they have critical gaps in all the other skills needed to successfully run a company.

In other words, the biggest weakness of first-time founders who have just left their job is that they are often functional experts in just one (or two) area(s).

And this can kill your business - sometimes even before it really gets off the ground.

This only real exception is if you're coming from a senior (or senior-ish) role where you were responsible for high-leverage, big picture decision making that required you to regularly work cross-functionally with different business units.

If so, this would have allowed you to see, at a high level, how different key moving parts of a company work together in order to produce a viable, sustainable business.

But most of you aren't leaving senior level positions with broad decision-making responsibilities to start your company.

WHAT CAN YOU DO TO BUILD THE MESH OF REQUIRED ENTREPRENEURIAL SKILLS?

And since most of you don't fall into this latter category, you better find ways to get the skills you need.

Here are some ways if you're a brand-new founder:

- Start a side-hustle, learn the ropes and get valuable market feedback with small-scale, low-cost experiments before quitting your job
- Read books or watch YouTube videos that specifically focus on on-the-ground tactics (not just high-level strategy or vague notions of "management") of generating awareness in the market, and how to turn those into leads and sales. For example, recommendations for marketing include Jay Abraham, Dan Kennedy and Joe Sugarman. Do the

appropriate research for who you need to seek out in areas where you're weak

- Take courses that have ideally force you to apply your knowledge with a capstone project so that you're not just mindlessly consuming with zero application
- Speak to mentors to learn from someone who's ahead of you in areas where you are weak and to shed further light on "known knowns", "known unknowns" and "unknown unknowns"

Out of the above list, I would put #1 and #2 as the most effective in helping you to fill any gaps in your skillset needed to run a viable business.

Consuming high ROI books and videos that teach you specific, on-the-ground tactical skills (such as copywriting and setting up sales funnels) will not only give you the immediate skills you need, but will also often unlock the "unknown unknowns" of bigger picture strategies (such as ways to use copywriting within the structure of your sales funnels in ways you may not have thought of before).

In many cases, these bigger picture strategies would not have been visible to you had you not gained certain on-the-ground skills in the first place.

Once you've done the above, take the skills you just learned and hone them in a real-world situation with your side business and learn from the ultimate teacher: the commercial marketplace.

My guess is that you'll find that having this safe learning period will ultimately be a lot more beneficial to your entrepreneurial success than quitting your job (and income) without key skills already in place.

CHAPTER 25
A SIMPLE, LIGHTWEIGHT 3-STEP FORMULA FOR FINDING YOUR PROFITABLE NICHE USING GROUP, PROBLEM AND SOLUTION

A simple, lightweight 3-step formula for finding your profitable niche:

- 👥 = Group of people
- ! = A problem they have and/or opportunity for them
- 💡 = Your solution

For example:

- 👥 = Operations managers at mid-sized supply chain companies in the iron ore industry
- ! = Who need help managing their communication with purchasing agents around the world
- 💡 = An API that integrates directly into Microsoft Teams and Slack

Now add them together and you get:

We help operations managers at mid-sized supply chain companies in the iron ore industry solve the problem of managing their communication with purchasing agents around the world via our API that integrates directly into their Microsoft Teams and Slack.

The more specific you can niche in 👥 , ❗ and 💡 the more likely you are to:

- Attract self-selecting leads (i.e. pre-qualified)
- Convert those leads into customers
- Convert freemium users into paying users

CHAPTER 26
ATTRACT MORE BUYERS WITH RESONANT NICHE, POSITIONING AND MESSAGING

The 3 steps to drawing in buyers like iron fillings to a magnet are correctly picking your Niche, Positioning and Messaging.

Why does this work?

Because your Niche influences your Positioning, which then influences your Messaging.

NICHING

Your Niche is a description of WHO you're selling to, the specific PROBLEM(S) they have and the WHAT of your solution.

- **Example:** *"Operations managers at mid-sized supply chain companies in the iron ore industry + Who need help managing their communication with purchasing agents around the world + an API that integrates directly into Microsoft Teams and Slack"*

(Let's call our solution "Minerva". And yes, you've seen me use this particular niching example before)

POSITIONING

Positioning takes the descriptive nature of the Niche, and packages it into a compelling, high-level marketing angle you communicate to your target audience of what it can OVERALL do for them and summed up in one or two sentences.

- **Example:** *"Minerva gives operations managers in the iron ore mining industry the ability to simply manage dozens of complex text, video and audio communications with third-party purchasing agents around the world using their existing internal tools"*

MESSAGING

Messaging includes the specific feature-related benefit(s) of your product and is derived from your Positioning.

In other words, it's the specific benefits embedded within your high-level Positioning.

Here's 3 examples of features-benefits messaging:

- **Message #1:** *"Minerva simplifies long, back-and-forth conversations by organizing them in individual threads, which means your team can ultimately handle a greater volume of conversations at the same time"*
- **Message #2:** *"Minerva integrates directly into your existing Microsoft Teams or Slack account which means you save subscription costs and onboarding expenses normally associated with the introduction of new tools"*
- **Message #3:** *"Minerva visually tracks the real-time movement and paperwork status of your iron ore shipments so that you can easily align conversations with purchasing agents as the shipments get unloaded at various global ports."*

HOW DO YOU KNOW IF YOUR NICHING, POSITIONING AND MESSAGING ARE WORKING?

Very easy - the most definitive measure is if people are paying you. And the more dialed in each of the three elements are, the more frequently and/or larger your individual sales are.

CHAPTER 27
WHY ARE CUSTOMERS FALLING OUT OF LOVE WITH YOUR PRODUCT?

When finding why a customer churned, ask yourself: "Why did my product stop being relevant to them?"

Just because your product was relevant at the point of purchase - and was still relevant yesterday doesn't mean it remains the same today.

Users can fall out of love (or no longer find utility) with your product for a number of reasons: a superior competitor, a bad experience with your team, a change in career or a life transition.

Churn isn't just something to be plugged like a leaky bucket with discounts and a reactive product roadmap - that's playing defense.

You also need to play offense by anticipating the types of challenges you can solve for them, and the opportunities you can create.

Ultimately, product stickiness is created by being relevant to your users right now and on an on-going basis with no breaks in continuity.

Stickiness is not created by falling into the pit of irrelevance, and then scrambling reactively with catch-up features to try to become relevant again to your users' lives.

Different users have different tolerances for this - some will cut you a bit of slack and stay subscribed while you sort things out, while others will leave right away.

But in either case, it's better to skate alongside (and ahead of) your users, rather than fall behind and trying to catch up afterwards.

Do that too many times and even your most forgiving users will leave you for your competitors.

And who's fault would that be?

CHAPTER 28
THE 3 PILLARS TO BEAT CHURN AND INCREASE USER RETENTION: UTILITY, SATISFACTION AND COMMUNICATION

Got churn issues?

That sucks.

Here's the simple 3-step framework I use with my clients to troubleshoot churn.

The 3 components of churn (and by extension, user retention) are:

1. Your product's relevant value exceeds price paid
2. Net positive user experience with your product and company
3. You communicate continued relevant value

YOUR PRODUCT'S RELEVANT VALUE EXCEEDS PRICE PAID

Of the 3 framework components, this has the highest influence on whether a customer sticks with you.

I'll break this component up into its constituent pieces for maximum clarity.

The question you need to ask yourself is:

- In the eyes of your buyer

- ...does your product solve problems (or create benefits) to the extent
- ...that the total perceived value they believe they are getting from your product
- ...is at least equal to the price they paid?

If the answer is no, they'll churn.

In other words, the price they're paying exceeds the total value they're getting back in the form of problems solved or benefits created.

It's important to look at this from the perspective of your buyer, and not how much value YOU think your product provides.

Your opinion of how much value you *think* your creation provides is irrelevant to your users and buyers. It's common for many founders to see their product through rose-tinted lenses, so beware.

NET POSITIVE USER EXPERIENCE WITH YOUR PRODUCT AND COMPANY

User satisfaction is the aggregate of your customer's current and past experiences with your company and product.

On the company side, this could be their experience with customer support (rude reps?), the contract (hidden fees?) or delivery (damaged goods?)

On the product side, this could be a difficult, unintuitive interface, frequent crashes or downtime.

Keep in mind that overall positive user satisfaction isn't just that positive experiences outnumbered negative experiences.

More important is to understand that different individual negative / positive experiences will carry different weights.

For example, a single instance of a data breach will outweigh (in fact, erase) the goodwill generated from multiple instances of fast, empathetic customer support service.

The ultimate question to ask here is: do your buyer's accumulated positive experiences exceed their accumulated negative experiences?

COMMUNICATING CONTINUED RELEVANT VALUE

This is the act of communicating your continued relevant value to your buyer.

The macro-environment (technology, economics, law, society, etc) evolve and customer preferences change as a result.

As you adapt your product by building capabilities that answer the challenges and opportunities of today and the near future, do you make sure to TELL your customers about these new features (and their benefits)?

This is a trap many product-centric founders fall into.

They myopically focus on their widget while forgetting to communicate the value of their widget to their customers and the market.

Make sure you're not just building a product that offers relevant value to your buyers - you must also tell them that you now offer this new relevant value.

If not, you might end up in a situation where a competitor builds features that offer the same (or similar) relevant value but tells the market (including YOUR customers) before you do.

This is an easy mistake to avoid. Make sure you tell your buyers and your market what new relevant value you've created for them. In the first case, you keep your current customers, and in the second, you potentially bring on new ones.

SUMMARY

- **Product Utility:** in the eyes of your buyer, does your product offer them total relevant value (in form of problems solved or benefits created) such that it exceeds the price they pay?

- **User Satisfaction:** do their accumulated positive experiences (with your company and product) outweigh their accumulated negative experiences?
- **Communication:** are you effectively telling your buyers about new features that offer them relevant value?

CHAPTER 29
IT'S NOT ENOUGH TO SIMPLY BE A CONTRARIAN THINKER

Contrarian thinking only pays off when you're contrarian AND right.

Instead, what you need to do is take intelligent, considered risks / opportunities while thinking through to (at least) the second-order consequences of those immediate actions.

Jumping off a cliff is no doubt contrarian thinking (you just need to do the exact opposite of everyone else, right?) - but I doubt you would reap much benefits from this particular type of contrarian thinking.

On the other hand: skipping college and channeling the money and time saved to get a head-start on learning sales and marketing, product development and other key business skills?

That's contrarian thinking (thankfully less so in recent years) AND right.

The key is in getting the qualifier "and right", well, right (more specifically, right for YOU.

Remember, you don't want to be contrarian for the sake of being contrarian.

Now in many cases it's hard to tell if your decision or action will ultimately turn out right - but sometimes it's obviously and plainly not right, so why the heck are you even doing it?

I've met more than my fair share of people who by *default* always "do the opposite of everyone else" because that's "jUsT hOw I aM".

For them it's an almost identity-level issue – i.e. "I will do the opposite because that's how I define myself"

(In other words, "I'm different and it's personally important to me to be different because it undergirds one of my core inner identities")

Frankly (and in my opinion) it's a bit of a stupid approach to life to knowingly adhere to any sort of rigid, dogmatic approach just for the sake of adhering to said rigid, dogmatic approach.

It's also an overly simplistic way of looking at the world - and a very wrong one that could produce very real negative consequences.

And don't also just reflexively "do the opposite of everyone else" because the latest and greatest rah-rah-rah popular business book or celebrity "thought leader" du jour tells you to (I have a few in mind, but I won't name names)

Take the risks you need, but make sure you're also doing it in intelligent, considered ways while thinking through to *at least* the second-order consequences of your immediate actions.

As a bootstrapped founder (particularly a first-time one) you probably have a lot less margin for error than others with a secure 9-to-5 job or those with cash in the bank from an exit.

CHAPTER 30
FIVE EXAMPLES OF MOVING BEYOND COMFORT ZONES FOR SUSTAINED BUSINESS SUCCESS

Breaking your comfort zones isn't enough for long-term business success.

The world changes quick.

Rather than pushing beyond your normal comfort zones, you must also change the way you see what's possible (your context).

Here are 5 examples to get you thinking about how to break into a new context for long-term business success.

BUSINESS CONSULTANT

- **Breaking comfort zone:** Charging higher per hourly rates with higher-end clients
- **Breaking context zone:** Productizing services with digital products (e-books, online courses, mastermind groups). Charging by percentage of improvement

SOFTWARE ENGINEER

- **Breaking comfort zone:** Learning new coding languages to take on more varied freelance gigs
- **Breaking context zone:** Flipping micro-SaaS. Building SaaS in days/weeks, getting handful of paid users and selling on specialized flipping marketplace. Rinse & repeat

RESTAURANT

- **Breaking comfort zone:** Adding more tables and expanded menu
- **Breaking context zone:** Switching the business model to a ghost kitchen (delivery-only, no dine-in) and selling pre-packaged versions of their menu via a DTC model

MEDICAL DOCTOR

- **Breaking comfort zone:** Expanding their practice by adding more doctors
- **Breaking context zone:** Adding membership-based services focused on preventative care (rather than the traditional fee-for-service model)

REAL ESTATE AGENT

- **Breaking comfort zone:** Expanding into new neighborhoods
- **Breaking context zone:** Transitioning into a real estate tech platform offering virtual house tours, digital transaction processes and AI-driven pricing insights

SUMMARY

- Breaking your comfort zone = pushing existing boundaries

- Breaking your contextual zone = changing the way you fundamentally see / do things
- Long-term success requires new contextual zones because the world is changing at increasing speed and complexity

CHAPTER 31
SURFACING NEW HIDDEN OPPORTUNITIES BY BREAKING OUT OF COMFORT ZONES INTO NEW CONTEXT ZONES

Business and life-changing growth lies in going beyond your context zones, and not just your comfort zones.

What's the difference between comfort and context zones? And why does it matter that you also need to break out of your current context zones?

BREAKING OUT OF COMFORT ZONES IS WHAT MOST PEOPLE DO

Going beyond your **comfort zone** would be cold DMing or cold-calling that Big Scary Enterprise Customer.

Or giving a keynote speech in front of 4,000 fellow entrepreneurs at a conference.

Piercing your comfort zone is doing something beyond your current skill set or level of courage in the realm of known knowns and known unknowns.

In other words, you're doing "more of more-or-less the same".

Which is what everyone else is chasing.

But if you want to distinguish yourself, you need to allocate some of your time and effort to doing things that are different AND which benefit you and your business.

WHAT IS GOING PAST YOUR CONTEXT ZONE?

Going beyond your **context zone** is something else entirely and it's doing things that exist outside your blind spots (unknown unknowns).

Here's an example that better explains this:

I once spoke to a senior decision-maker at a large regional American food and beverage chain. Our discussion was around the thin margins, high competition and overall difficulty of operating in this space.

What could they do to generate more revenue while increasing net profit margins WITHOUT increasing capital expenditure?

Had we stayed within our existing contextual zones, we might have come up with the usual answers: extend operating hours, add higher priced menu options, downsize portion sizes, buy cheaper ingredients or cut staff.

But in expanding beyond our context zones, we came up with:

- Acting as a broker of funding relationships for other restaurants
- Licensing their operating model to restaurants outside their geography, including internationally (everywhere outside North America)

How did we come up with these two ideas?

First, this chain enjoyed impeccable relationships with financial institutions. I proposed that they could act as an intermediary for other restaurant chains that needed access to capital.

This food and beverage group could make the introductions and take a percentage for facilitating the transaction. It would be a win-win for the borrower, the lender and this chain.

Second, because of well-defined and honed Standard Operating Procedures (SOPs), this group had far higher than average profit margin than its competitors.

I proposed they could package some (or all) of their SOPs into a specialized information product (or service) and charge a very high license fee for other restaurants who wanted to learn what made a high-margin restaurant tick.

What made this revenue engine even better was that it was extremely scalable because it was a highly niched product that could be replicated at no (or little) additional marginal cost and could be sold all over the world at the click of a button.

That's breaking out of your context zones.

SUMMARY

If you just break out of your comfort zones (known knowns and known unknowns), you'll just be doing more of what you already know, at a higher level.

But when you break out of your context zones (unknown unknowns), you can completely change the game and generate highly profitable, extremely scalable opportunities that are completely invisible to your competition.

And who doesn't like having an unfair advantage?

What are examples of you breaking out of your comfort zone? And examples of breaking out of your context zones?

CHAPTER 32
SEVEN KEY PEOPLE YOU MAY ENCOUNTER DURING YOUR B2B SALE

Depending on the scale and complexity of your B2B sale, you may or may not encounter all of these people, but it's worth keeping all of these personas in mind.

ECONOMIC BUYER

This person owns the budget and assesses whether the purchase makes sense from financial and ROI points of view.

DECIDER

They decide whether to proceed with the purchase itself.

Will often be the same person as the Economic Buyer (though not always the case).

END USER

They will be the ones using the product on a daily (or at least regular or semi-regular) basis.

INFLUENCER

They influence the purchase with their opinions and assessments of your product (which may be positive or negative).

The Influencer often overlaps with the End User and has the necessary expertise to provide a credible assessment for their colleagues.

CHAMPION

A subset of the Influencer. Someone who (for professional or personal reasons) supports adopting your product and will actively lobby for it.

In other words, your internal advocate at your prospect's company.

Make this person your best friend.

TECHNICAL BUYER

For solutions that require implementation (for eg. integration, security, scalability, data migration etc), this person assesses your product from a technical point of view.

They are another subset of the Influencer.

GATEKEEPER

Controls access to key people on the customer-side.

The Gatekeeper could be a secretary, receptionist or executive assistant.

Make sure you're on their good side or you can find yourself locked out of key relationships to close the sale.

SUMMARY

These are the 7 people you will encounter during a B2B sale.

1. Economic Buyer
2. Decider

3. End User
4. Influencer
5. Champion
6. Technical Buyer
7. Gatekeeper

CHAPTER 33
WHY YOU DON'T NEED TO ALWAYS CHASE "BIG BANG" INNOVATIONS FOR SUCCESS

Yes, you can create money-making innovations for your business right now.

Creating money-making innovations right now? That's a big promise!

Here's how you do it: by not thinking of "innovation" as just industry or world-changing ideas such as AI, blockchain or AR/VR.

Instead, innovation is anything that improves the experience of your:

- Prospect
- Customer
- Team

And they don't need to be big improvements.

Small, simple improvements can be innovations that make a noticeable change to your business.

Three examples of prospect, customer and team-focused innovation:

1. An improved landing page that more clearly spells out the benefits, features of your product

2. New payment plans (pay quarterly) and methods (for eg. crypto)
3. New project management software

Example 1 is prospect-focused innovation. The second is customer-focused innovation. The third is team-focused innovation.

Don't let "innovation" as it's commonly portrayed scare you from making small improvements that materially improve your revenue and profit margins.

In fact, you're probably better off implementing a number of small innovations rather than trying to hit one giant home run.

If you improve 3 areas of your company by just 10%, you improve the entire business by 33%.

Much easier than try to get a 33% improvement in one area alone.

Sure, go for the big home runs if you want.

But don't forget the low-hanging fruit as well.

CHAPTER 34
THE REASON YOU DON'T CLOSE MORE SALES

The reason you don't enjoy more sales is because you fail to show people how your product gives them a new, better future.

Sales people call this tactic "future pacing".

Maybe a simpler way is to call this "good business sense".

CHAPTER 35
WHY MAKING IT EASY FOR OTHERS IS THE GOLDEN RULE OF FAVOR-ASKING

One really easy shortcut to relationship success is to make it easy for the other person when you're asking a favor of them.

If you're asking your friend or ex-colleague for an introduction to a prospect, send them a pre-written introduction instead of expecting your contact to do the heavy lifting and write it themselves.

If you WhatsApp or text someone to ask for information, don't just leave it at "Got a sec?" (you know who you are).

Instead, actually include what your request is.

In other words, JUST ASK THE QUESTION YOU WANT ANSWERED.

Yes, just get to the point and ask!

For example:

"Got a sec? Wanted to double check if you knew Bob Smith of Salesforce - was hoping you could quickly fill me in on him as I've got a meeting with him next week. Understand that you used to work together."

If you ask a contact to review something (such as a contract or landing page), then either point out or outline the provisions or areas you would like them to comment on.

Don't just expect them to figure it out on their own when they're the ones doing YOU the favor.

It only takes you a few extra moments to make it easier for the other person. If you do, you can maintain (and perhaps grow) the relationship.

Make it hard for the other person (especially a busy one) too many times, and they'll want to stop dealing with you.

And that could have been easily avoided if you just did the extra little leg work yourself.

CHAPTER 36
IT'S EASY TO MAKE BIG PROMISES TO PROSPECTS, BUT IT'S HARDER TO KEEP THEM

It's easy to make big promises to prospects. But can you deliver?

More importantly, can you overdeliver to the extent that they want an ongoing, medium or long-term relationship with you?

Underdeliver = bye-bye
Deliver = open to trying competitors
Overdeliver = they stick with you

CHAPTER 37
TURN MORE PROSPECTS INTO CUSTOMERS: A 3-STEP FRAMEWORK FOR HELPING PROSPECTS ENVISION THEIR DESIRED FUTURES AND OVERCOME SELF-DOUBT

Raise your number of sales and sign-ups with this 3-step marketing framework that you can use on landing pages, ads and social media.

Here's the 3 components you need to know:

- Build your prospect's desire for your product
- Overcome doubts and uncertainty they have about themselves
- Help them imagine themselves experiencing the full benefits of having already used your product

Here's a breakdown of each step:

BUILD THEIR DESIRE FOR YOUR PRODUCT

Your prospect may be discovering you for the first time and know little about either your brand or product. Your job in Step 1 is to build their desire for your offering, and then amplify that desire in the here-and-now.

Use things like high-quality imagery and video, endorsements, testi-monials/case studies and compelling sales copy that focuses on your product's benefits (ie. positive implications), not just the features.

Ever wonder why you start salivating and always seem to want to drive down to the local McDonald's after watching an ad for Big Macs?

Well, the close-up shots of the sizzling 100% beef patty, crisp lettuce and ripe, juicy tomatoes with tangy special sauce sandwiched between two perfectly perfect sesame seed buns probably had something to do with it.

Then pair all of the above with more close-ups shots: this time of a large, overflowing cup of icy Coca-Cola and crispy, "just right" golden straight-cut fries tumbling out of the iconic red McDonald's container.

Plus, it didn't hurt to have McDonald's pay millions of dollars to Michael Jordan, Heidi Klum and BTS to eat this stuff as official "brand ambassadors" (ie. celebrity endorsers).

And now you know how to leverage Step 1.

OVERCOME DOUBTS AND UNCERTAINTY ABOUT THEMSELVES

It's not that your product isn't great - I'm sure it is.

But often what holds people back from buying and using something is because they have their own personal reasons for why they don't see themselves as "the right person" for your offering.

For example, the root cause that holds many people back from joining (and then consistently going) to the gym is not just that they are uncomfortable with how they currently look - but it has more so to do with the much deeper reason of feeling they will be judged by others.

It is what they feel on this deeper level which drives their actions (or lack of action) – and this is what you need to address.

In other words, your job as a founder, marketer and salesperson is to ALSO help your prospect overcome their doubts and uncertainties they have about THEMSELVES being suitable FOR YOUR OFFERING – not the other way around.

If you did Step 1 correctly, they already see the product as the right choice for them, but they also need to see themselves as the right choice for your product.

So maybe you organize gym classes three times a week that are open exclusively to new joiners. The intention is that they can work out in an environment that is as non-judgmental as possible until they get their sea legs (so to speak).

Or perhaps you set aside a physical space that is for "newbies only".

But Step 2 is basically anything to help your prospect say "Yes, I clearly see myself buying and using this product or service. I see that I am suitable for this offering and this offering is suitable for me."

HELP THEM IMAGINE THEMSELVES EXPERIENCING THE FULL BENEFITS OF HAVING ALREADY USED YOUR PRODUCT

The final step is to (to the full extent you can) "future pace" your prospect - i.e. paint a compelling future for them in which they not only see, but ideally experience, themselves fully enjoying the comprehensive benefits of having already used your product.

This would include not only the immediate product-based benefits derived from using your offering, but also the ancillary benefits that consequently flow from it on a physical, emotional, psychological and spiritual level.

If you are an owner of a resort in Bali, you could do the above by making your prospect feel this:

> *"You step onto the veranda of your 3rd story suite, drinking in the verdant green vista of tropical foliage in front of you, framed between the sunlight skies of mid-afternoon and the shimmering, turquoise waters of the sandy bay.*
>
> *Behind you quietly slips in the resort attendant bearing a large spread of the*

choicest tropical fruits - pungent, creamy durians, succulent, melt-in-your-mouth mangos and sugary, thirst-quenching guavas.

This is the prize for your years of entrepreneurship grind - the late nights, rejections by prospects and near brushes with financial death. But unlike others, you emerged fully victorious - and here you are, living and reveling in a life open only to the small minority who successfully made it through a combination of hard work, grind and wits.

You are part of a small, select group and you deserve every part of today."

In effect, we are taking Step 1 (Build their desire for your product) and putting it on steroids by not only amplifying the immediate benefits of using your product, but taking the prospect by the hand and vividly painting for them the medium and long-term lifestyle they could unlock if only they bought your offering.

Give this 3-step framework a try. I think you'll be pleasantly surprised by how well it works to get your prospects excited about buying what you're selling.

CHAPTER 38
WHY SMART FOUNDERS CHOOSE TO OWN, NOT RENT, THEIR CUSTOMER DATA

Do you think you actually own your company's customer list on LinkedIn, Instagram, YouTube, or another platform?

Any of these platforms can suspend your account - either for cause, or accidentally.

For example, there was at least one documented instance of Instagram locking thousands of users out of their accounts due to a glitch.

Platforms constantly change what behavior can lead to account suspensions - or worse, outright bans.

In other words, if you have put a lot of time and effort into growing your following, you may wish to reconsider whether you actually own your customer list.

And you're not safe either on platforms such as Substack that bill themselves as business- and creator-friendly because they allow you to download your followers' email addresses.

You can still get suspended without notice and locked out of your hard-earned customer list.

These are all examples of "rented lists" - ie. you merely have access to your customers at the whim and pleasure of the platform.

Make sure you're saving your customer details in your own databases by regularly downloading your customers' contact details from your accounts.

Or, if that's not possible, driving traffic to your own landing pages where you can capture their details.

Then you'll no longer rent your customer lists, but actually own them for *real*.

And that's one of the steps to building a resilient business with true redundancy.

CHAPTER 39
A PROSPECT'S WILLINGNESS TO PAY FOR SOLUTIONS DOESN'T MEAN THEY WILL BUY YOURS

In any sale, make sure a prospect's willingness to pay is not just a general willingness to pay for solutions in your space, but a specific willingness to pay for YOUR solution.

CHAPTER 40
WHY SALES SUCCESS IS MORE THAN WORDS AND HOW YOUR EMOTIONAL STATE SPEAKS VOLUMES

Heading into a sales meeting after a tough morning or afternoon?

Clear your emotional state before walking into the conference room or jumping on that video call.

Prospects can pick up on your underlying non-verbal state and it matters - even if you have a great product that produces the exact desired benefits they seek.

While it may not ultimately sink your sale, you always want to stack the deck in your favor as much as possible.

In sales, it can be difficult to predict when you need every single advantage, no matter how small.

All it takes is a minute or two to leave your frustration at the door before starting your sales call.

Remember that it's not just what you say (and how you say it), but also the non-verbal sub-communication that undergirds your presence.

CHAPTER 41
BUSINESS ETIQUETTE CHANGES WHEN SELLING AROUND THE WORLD, BUT YOUR OUTCOMES SHOULDN'T

I've split my life between North America and Asia. People ask me whether I prefer business etiquette from one part of the world over another.

How I behave for meetings in Asia (using English, Cantonese and Mandarin):

1. Bow when accepting business cards (only from the neck for about 10 degrees - I don't bow from the hip)
2. Accept cards with both hands
3. Study each card for a moment as I receive them
4. Arrange all cards face-up on the table when seated
5. Line cards horizontally (never vertically so that I don't accidentally put the card of someone more junior above someone senior)
6. Use of honorifics (Mr / Ms) unless they first use my given name
7. Deliberately calibrate the loudness of my voice, tone and speaking speed to be slightly deferential if speaking to someone older
8. Body language deliberately more restrained and controlled

For meetings in North America:

1. No bowing
2. Accept business cards with one hand
3. Pocket the cards
4. Acceptable (and expected) to converse on a first-name basis
5. Use my normal voice and body language regardless of the other person's age or seniority

Which is best?

Neither.

The "best way" is whatever gets (and keeps) business for the particular context you're operating in at the moment.

CHAPTER 42
IF A PRODUCT GETS MADE AND NO ONE IS AROUND TO KNOW ABOUT IT, DOES IT REALLY EXIST?

Making a perfectly perfect product doesn't mean people will buy.

Money only starts flowing when you tell buyers:

- Your product exists
- Its measurable benefits for them
- Why they should pick you over competitors

CHAPTER 43
WHY IGNORING MARKET ALTERNATIVES COULD BE A BIG SALES MISTAKE

It might not be a direct competitor who steals your sale, but an alternative.

How might a market alternative steal your sale?

Here's an example:

- **Direct competitors** = Coke vs Pepsi. They vie for the same market.
- **Alternatives to Coke/Pepsi** = Water, juice or tea. These are products which target another market but can all solve the same core problem.

The lesson? Know who else your buyer looks to for solutions.

CHAPTER 44
A FRAMEWORK TO BUILD PRODUCTS THAT RESONATE WITH YOUR TARGET AUDIENCE BY DELIVERING THEIR DESIRED OUTCOMES

As founders, how do we determine what creates value for users and buyers?

The solution to this question is to think about what kind of desired outcomes users and buyers (who are not necessarily the same group) want, and then to add features, services and/or experiences to fulfill these desired outcomes.

WHAT ARE DESIRED OUTCOMES?

By "desired outcomes" I mean those that:

- Solve their current problem(s)
- Solve their anticipated problem(s)
- Generate future opportunities that they want
- Fulfill a need or want (for eg. hardcore golf aficionados don't have problems to be solved per se, but they do have a want for the latest and greatest golf technology)

Often desired outcomes belong to the categories of:

- Health
- Wealth
- Relationships

These can then be further broken down into the subcategories of:

- Convenience (ease of doing - for eg. effortlessly find a romantic partner)
- Savings (scoop out more of from a *fixed* pie – for eg. time)
- Enhancement (create more of with no limit to the upside – for eg. money)

Ideally, it is only your product that can create these desired outcomes - this is when you can really make it rain money with a monopoly.

IT'S IMPORTANT TO FOCUS ON THE "DESIRED" PART OF "DESIRED OUTCOMES"

Why?

Because you can solve a problem or create an opportunity that doesn't benefit them in the way *they want*.

An example is solving a customer's termite problem by burning down their house.

You've gotten rid of their termites alright, but not in a way that they want (unless they're weirdos).

The other possibility is that you create outcomes that either aren't important and/or aren't relevant to them.

There's a distinction between important and relevant.

Important means that the issue has some sort of significant consequential bearing on their lives.

Relevant means whether they care about the issue.

Here's are examples to explain:

- **Important + Relevant** = Feeling pain in your left chest (could be a heart attack)
- **Important + Irrelevant** = Failing your medical school exams, but you don't care because you were going to drop out anyway to become an artist
- **Unimportant + Relevant** = Deciding between pizza or bibimbap for lunch
- **Unimportant + Irrelevant** = What your next-door neighbor had for lunch

IS IMPORTANCE OR RELEVANCE MORE IMPORTANT?

I would say that the bigger test to watch out for in the immediate term is whether something is relevant to your buyer or user.

What they care about in the here and now they will take action on - and what they don't care about, they won't - no matter how important.

An example that deftly illustrates relevance (or lack thereof) are the large number of high school kids these days pumping themselves full of steroids.

The prospect of major health problems (including organ failure) is just too far removed into the future so it's not relevant to them in the here and now even though it's deathly important (literally)

SUMMARY

Don't start by thinking of exact features or capabilities to add. Instead, begin by considering what outcomes your users and/or buyers desire.

Then come up with features, services and experiences that answer the following questions:

- **For prospects:** What is it that will benefit my prospect such that they want to start doing business with me?"
- **For existing customers:** "What is it that will benefit my client such that they will want to continue doing business with me and/or do more business with me?"

In other words, value in a product comes not necessarily from features per se, but features that solve problems that matter to users and buyers.

Using the above framework as the foundation of your thinking, you can then expansively generate (whether in-house or in partnership with others) completely new offerings (or enhancements to existing offerings) that ultimately benefit your prospect and/or customer.

Give it a try.

CHAPTER 45
WHY EVERY TECHNICAL FOUNDER NEEDS TO MASTER THE ART OF SELLING TO EMOTIONS

Founders with highly technical backgrounds often don't know - or forget - that a big part of effective selling is communicating to the prospect's emotions.

In other words, they often overlook the fact that they are ultimately selling to human beings, and that our primal "lizard brain" is always active, lurking just below the surface.

These founders often disgorge a bunch of technically correct facts, figures and assertions about their products' capabilities.

MAKE YOUR PITCHES MORE EFFECTIVE BY SPEAKING TO A PROSPECT'S EMOTION

To really amplify the effectiveness of their pitches, founders should also paint pictures of what their prospect's future looks like without the product - and what it would look like with it.

In other words, using storytelling to paint a compelling future of how the prospect's life will be improved.

In doing so, they can also layer in "away" and "towards" triggers to ensure they speak to both kinds of human motivation.

"Away" motivational triggers include scarcity or FOMO (Fear of Missing Out).

"Towards" motivational triggers include belonging, humor, nostalgia or luxury.

It's up to you to decide what you want to use - and how much of each to use - but amplifying your pitch with away and towards emotions is much more effective than merely reciting facts.

As a journalist turned legal practitioner who loved getting technical with the law, layering emotion into my pitches was something I had to relearn.

For other technically minded founders, it's something well worth your time to learn (or relearn).

Communicating to your prospects' and customers' emotions will make sales easier and contracts stickier.

Don't just talk to your prospect or customer - talk to the human being behind the prospect and customer.

Give it a try.

CHAPTER 46
FROM OVERLOOKED TO OVERBOOKED WITH OPPORTUNITY: THE POWER OF PROMPT REPLIES IN BUILDING TRUST

One of the most underrated skills in business (and life) is simply being able to close the loop with people so you don't leave them hanging.

Simply being able to reply back to people within a few hours or (at most) a few days so you resolve their uncertainty of waiting for your answer is kind of a super power in business and life.

But a surprising number of people don't (or can't) do this, so use it to your advantage.

Humans hate being left hanging, so even if you get back to your business and personal relationships with a simple "no", it'll put you miles ahead of the competition.

I don't know about you, but I love having an unfair advantage - especially when this one is so easy to apply to generate tangible, real-world results.

ENTIRE LUCRATIVE INDUSTRIES WITH HIGHLY PAID STAFF HAVE BEEN BUILT ON THIS CONCEPT OF CLOSING THE LOOP QUICKLY

These money-making organizations include the fastest moving firms in tech, law, finance and strategy consulting.

And in relationship-driven *service* businesses, this is a MUST - particularly when the product you're selling isn't something you can openly show (or talk about) in order to demonstrate to prospects your superiority over the competition.

For example, Apple can demonstrate to their prospects greater skill, value, utility and judgment over Samsung by comparing, point-by-point, the openly disclosed and plainly visible features of the iPhone with those of Samsung equivalents (for eg. more storage space, higher megapixel camera, higher resolution screen, etc).

(The same is true when Samsung wants to demonstrates superiority over iPhones)

But certain service businesses like law firms can't openly share with a prospect the end-deliverables (restricted information) they sell.

For instance, a law firm can't share a confidential Share Purchase Agreement (SPA) they drafted for a previous client and compare it with another SPA drafted by another law firm to demonstrate their own greater skill, value, utility and judgment.

This is why "responsiveness" (actually, hyper-responsiveness) is a sine qua non of law firms, accounting firms and other service businesses.

And it's also one reason why the *top* firms are so successful.

A lawyer who gets a client's query at midnight might not have the answer right away, but it would be in their interest to send something like "I don't yet have the exact answer for you, but I just wanted you to know we're on it" to the client right away.

BE AS RESPONSIVE AS YOU WANT - JUST KNOW THAT CLIENTS AND PROSPECTS JUDGE YOUR ACCORDINGLY

Now, you don't have to take it to the same extremes as the most relationship-driven service businesses, but you DO want some level of responsiveness that is superior to your competition.

And believe me - people ARE silently deciding whether to work with you by your responsiveness.

And here's another thing – if you can't be counted on to reply when times are good, can people count on you to reply (or communicate) when things go awry?

It's not hard to be responsive. For many of your professional relationships, your ability to do so (or not) speak volumes about how reliable, trust-worthy and safe they feel you are to work with.

Don't snatch defeat from the jaws of victory when this is such an easy fix.

CHAPTER 47
DON'T GIVE DISCOUNTS WITHOUT GETTING SOMETHING BACK

You'll inevitably get asked to give a discount by a client or prospect. You can do it, but here's what you can ask them for in exchange:

- Referrals
- Testimonials
- Signing a longer deal
- Appearing on your podcast
- Upfront payment on entire deal

Nearly everything is negotiable. Don't be surprised by what you can get if you ask confidently.

CHAPTER 48
THE MANTRA "SALES CURES ALL" IS WRONG, AND HERE'S WHY

Ok, so the mantra "Sales Cures All" isn't completely wrong - but it's only partially right at best.

Instead, the combination of CASH FLOW and CASH ACCESS cure all.

WHY DOES CASH FLOW AND CASH ACCESS CURE ALL WHILE SALES DOESN'T?

Sales cures all ONLY when those sales generate cash coming in - i.e. cash FLOW.

Sales classified under accounts receivable - where you deliver your product or service now and expect to get paid later - is an I.O.U. with you on the weaker side in the balance of power.

In other words, it's a promise by your buyer to hand over cash at a later date.

It is not cash in the bank or cash in hand.

And as some of you know, promises made are not always promises kept.

Therefore, don't operate under the simplistic assumption that "sALeS cUrEs all"

Because it doesn't.

And while big sales numbers are nice, you could make all the sales you want and still go bust if you don't have enough immediate cash flow (which directly impacts cash on hand) to pay your short-term obligations.

How are you going to pay the electric company to keep the lights on and pay your employees' salaries? Or how about the interest on the commercial loan you took out?

That's why you want effective cash COLLECTION to guarantee cash FLOW to build up cash ON HAND.

Ideally, you don't want a bunch of customer I.O.U.s (i.e. "We promise to pay you - or not")

CASH FLOW BY ITSELF ISN'T ENOUGH - YOU ALSO NEED TO BE ABLE TO ACCESS IT TOO

As we've seen with bank collapses from the past, you not only want cash flow, but ready ACCESS to cash (i.e. you can get to it when needed).

Cash flow is no good when you're locked out of it - or worse, when it goes poof into thin air.

The point of this post?

Sales doesn't cure all, but cash FLOW and cash ACCESS sure as hell can cure a lot. It's a good lesson for new business owners to keep in mind.

CHAPTER 49
TEN BUSINESS CONCEPTS EVERY SCHOOL SHOULD TEACH (BUT SADLY DON'T)

Instead of learning about different types of clouds (nimbus, cumulus) and rocks (igneous, sedimentary), this is what I wish I had been taught in school instead:

- Negotiation
- The 80/20 Rule
- Opportunity Cost
- Basic Accounting
- Compound Interest
- Supply and Demand
- Marketing and Branding
- How to Disagree Respectfully
- Instilling Accountability in Oneself and a Team
- How to Cold-Approach Potential Business Partners

Anything missing from this list that you would add?

CHAPTER 50
FIVE BUYING TRIGGERS TO ACCELERATE SALES, RAISE PERCEIVED VALUE, AND ENHANCE LOYALTY

Try these psychological triggers to make prospects more eager to buy, to buy more quickly, to buy more frequently and to buy at higher prices.

RAISE THE BUYER'S SOCIAL STATUS

Increase the buyer's real or perceived social standing by leveraging their human desire for more:

- Power
- Respect
- Influence
- Recognition

Example - Apple products such as the MacBook, iPhone or Apple Watch are equated with:

- Creativity
- Good taste
- Sophistication
- High performance
- Being on trend with current design & tech trends

Advantages:

- Can command a significant price premium since jockeying for social status is hardwired into all humans regardless of their ambition
- Generate strong buyer loyalty for the same reason as above

HARNESS SOCIAL PROOF

Leverage others' opinions to influence buying decisions.

The higher the real or perceived status of the other person, the more effective this is.

All of us have at least one area of life where we look to others to validate our choices / potential choices.

Example - For prospects, Amazon product reviews:

- Reduce perceived risk and doubt
- Give instant decision-making confidence
- Circumvent need to do the hard work of manual research

Advantages:

- Instantly builds trust
- Lets your customers do the selling for you
- Allows you to stack together dozens (if not more) 3rd-party validations of your product
- Perceived as more impartial (and thus, more truthful) than your sales material

LEVERAGE "US VERSUS THEM"

Create a sense of exclusivity and loyalty by encouraging buyers to identify with qualities valued by our in-group ("us") versus undesired out-groups ("them").

. . .

Example - Slack vs Microsoft Teams:

- Casual vs formal
- Agile vs traditional
- Open integration w/ 3rd-party apps vs more of a "walled garden"

Advantages:

- Less likely to churn because of higher than average level of loyalty
- Strong word-of-mouth as mere buyers are turned into devoted, evangelical advocates
- Increased customer responsiveness to buying new products and services

EXPLOIT SCARCITY

Drive more and faster sales by limiting availability of a product to raise its perceived value.

We are especially vulnerable because we:

- Desire what we can't have
- Fear disadvantaging ourselves to others who successfully buy and use it

Examples:

- **Rolex:** strict control over annual production of watches so that demand always exceeds supply
- **Starbucks:** limited time seasonal drinks such as Pumpkin Spice Latte
- **Expedia:** shows the number of rooms left at a given price

TAP INTO CURIOSITY AND NOVELTY

Tap into our desire to seek out new and interesting things.

Also leverages our desire to discover more by "pulling back the curtain".

Examples:

- **Apple:** creates suspense for new products with teaser ads and cryptic news releases
- **Taco Bell:** "Mystery Item" campaign used suspense-laden 15-second trailers leading up to the 2016 NFL Super Bowl

Advantages:

- Creates powerful viral sharing from ongoing buzz and word-of-mouth
- Ignites higher than average exploration from consumers who "want to know more"
- Increases brand memorability by exploiting power of unanswered questions ("open mental loops")

SUMMARY

Five buying triggers to accelerate sales, raise perceived value and enhance loyalty:

1. Raise the buyer's social status
2. Harness social proof
3. Leverage "Us versus them"
4. Exploit scarcity
5. Tap into curiosity and novelty

CHAPTER 51
THE MYTH OF SELLING BENEFITS: WHAT ACTUALLY WORKS WHEN SELLING OUTCOMES

Decades of traditional sales and marketing has wrongly told you that it's enough to simply list the different benefits of your product to prospects.

Just communicating general benefits (even if done well) doesn't work.

Why?

Because selling benefits to prospects is most effective when you concentrate on the ones that speak directly to an explicit need that they have said they have.

People don't buy *potential* pay-offs.

They instead buy to get pay-offs that can actually resolve or improve an issue they're personally dealing with.

Therefore, you don't need to tell your prospect all the possible benefits that your product has.

Just focus on the ones that can improve/resolve needs and desires they've explicitly told you about.

All other benefits you're so eager to communicate are superfluous.

CHAPTER 52
WHAT IF TAPPING INTO EMOTIONAL WANTS IS THE MISSING LINK IN YOUR SALES STRATEGY?

The easiest way to sell more is not to give people what they need - but what they want.

You yourself already understand deep down that people listen to their emotion-driven wants a lot more than their more logically-based needs.

DO YOU PREFER THE SLICE OF INDULGENT DOUBLE FUDGE CHOCOLATE CAKE (YUM) OR THE MUCH HEALTHIER BOWL OF BOILED CARROTS (BLEH)?

I already know which you're going to pick and I'm no mind reader.

What people want and what they need is often different.

And sometimes people can know one, but not the other.

Now, wants and needs do often align and that's when you have the most powerful buying trigger.

But sometimes you have a prospect that's just sitting on the fence.

Maybe they're blocked by their logical brain – ie. the one that's quietly (and correctly) admonishing your prospect, "But you don't NEED this Rolex watch."

And in this case, you would be remiss in your role as a founder, marketer and salesperson to ignore the power of wants (usually based in emotion) over needs (often rooted more so in logic).

By the way, I'm not saying you would be remiss to not USE the power of wants – I'm instead saying you would be remiss to IGNORE its power.

With that clarified, you would want - where the circumstances are appropriate - to press the emotional gas pedal of wants, not just lean exclusively on trying to further convince from a logical needs-based perspective.

EVER WONDER WHY YOU WASTE HOURS PROCRASTINATING BY WATCHING TRASHY YOUTUBE VIDEOS OVER INVESTING THAT TIME GETTING IN SHAPE, STARTING A BUSINESS OR LEARNING A USEFUL SKILL?

Because it feels GOOD to have your brain release little squirts of dopamine while you blow your time watching idiotic cat videos, someone gorging themselves with mukbang or someone streaming the newest video game on Twitch.

And as humans, we are inclined (or, designed) to do things that make us feel short-term pleasure over things that we know are actually beneficial, but which involve concentration, careful practice, frustration and pain.

But we don't need to stay in the realm of extreme examples to see that emotional wants are more powerful, effective sales triggers than logical needs.

Here's a few that you (or someone you know) has probably fallen victim to:

- Buying an expensive mechanical wristwatch (conveys status and prestige) over a cheap $15 plastic Casio that actually keeps better time and has more functionality[1]
- Buying a top-end Macbook Pro not because you need the

processing power or battery-life but because you "like how it makes you look when you work in crowded coffee shops"

- Showing off expensive restaurant meals on social media not because you're a creator and this is your business or genuine hobby, but because you want to flex to your friends

USE YOUR JUDGMENT IN LEVERAGING EMOTION AND IN FINE-TUNING IT

You know what? I think all of the above are perfectly fine as long as you're conscious you're being guided by your impulsive wants.

And frankly, on top of that, I'm writing this from the perspective of someone who helps founders increase their sales and profitability, so I'm not one to pass judgment.

In fact, it benefits my clients when people tap deeply into their wants, not just their needs.

But what I want to say is that, as a founder and entrepreneur, you need to learn there is a time and place for using all the tools in your toolkit.

And one of the most powerful tools you have is knowing when (and when not) to story-tell and convince from an emotional wants-based perspective, when to do so from a logical needs-based one and when to combine the two.

Use your best judgment as a founder to grow your business while being conscious of the power of the knowledge you possess.

---

1. Sometimes, what seem like purely emotional wants are in fact truly grounded in logic. For instance, certain professions (eg. banking and law) do in fact immensely benefit (more than the average) from conveying status and prestige to their clientele. I speak as someone who worked in law.

CHAPTER 53
YOU CAN SELL AT A LOSS IF YOU UNDERSTAND THESE 5 FACTORS

It's ok to sell at a loss if you know it will be made up by profitable return sales. But you must know:

- Your margins
- Average number of downstream sales
- If similar, cheaper products exist
- Likelihood of that client profile returning
- How long you can financially sustain this

And the most important thing to know is WHY you're selling at loss.

Is it to get your foot in the door with a particular market segment? Is it to grow market share?

Make sure you know your reason why.

CHAPTER 54
GIVING UP THE IDEA OF A MONDAY TO FRIDAY WORKWEEK MAY BE ONE OF YOUR MOST CONSEQUENTIAL DECISIONS

Friends, family and social media telling you that you need more work-life balance?

Consider opening up all seven days to the possibility of working - or resting (or playing).

In other words, your work is no longer time-boxed from Mondays to Fridays, and your rest and recharge periods are no longer limited to Saturdays and Sundays.

Rather, you work when you need (or want) to work, and you take time off when you need (or want).

This way, you escape putting artificial constraints on when and when not you are productive or resting.

Give it a try this weekend.

CHAPTER 55
DEBUNKING THE MYTH OF BRAND MARKETING: WHY EARLY-STAGE STARTUPS SHOULD STEER CLEAR

You're wasting your advertising money if you're only (or overly) focused on visual aesthetics and the cleverness of your copy.

As an early-stage startup, your main marketing goal isn't to win awards for design or eloquence.

Instead, your goal is to get the highest ROI on every single dollar you spend marketing your product to your target audience.

So don't try to get clever with Super Bowl-style ads. Leave that to the big corporate behemoths like Amazon, Volkswagen, Dell and Budweiser who have the money to spare.

For you, doing Super Bowl-style brand advertising is like loading up a wheelbarrow of cash and dumping that into your gas fireplace.

You wouldn't do that, right?

(I certainly wouldn't).

AS AN EARLY-STAGE STARTUP, YOU NEED TO BE LASER FOCUSED ON WHAT WORKS IN MARKETING

What's been proven to work over and over again in advertising are ads that use plain language to build desire for your product and contain *relevant* visuals (ie. don't show pictures of Boeing 747s flying over the Atlantic if you're selling bike tours in Tuscany).

Just as important is a simple, clear and directive CTA (Call to Action).

Three examples:

- *Click here to sign up for our free webinar on how to increase your sales by as much as 35% using our project management analytics API*
- *Join the lowest cost commodities trading platform with real-time updates of oil shipments throughout Southeast Asia and the Middle East*
- *Press the Join button to save 5+ hours a week by joining our meal prep delivery service*

Let your competitors be the ones haplessly and stupidly killing their cash runway with little to show for it.

For you, do what is most cost effective, cost efficient and which returns real-world results (ie. sales[1])

---

1. Ideally sales that are immediately cash flowing and not just sales on credit (ie. accounts receivable).

CHAPTER 56
BALANCING "WHO" AND "WHAT" YOU KNOW FOR NETWORKING SUCCESS

When I was in college, I used to think that "who you know" was all that mattered.

Relying only on "who you know" is too simplistic of a way to operate.

Rather, it's what you know AND who you know.

Who you know is heavily influenced by what you know.

More specifically, it's offering what you know that is relevant to those you want to know.

How can you offer value to those you want to know?

HERE'S A FEW WAYS TO OFFER VALUE TO THOSE YOU KNOW USING WHAT YOU KNOW

- Offer expertise and insights that are relevant. It doesn't have to be business-related either. Information related to hobbies can be equally helpful to build relationships
- Make introductions. There may be people or opportunities in which you can act as a middle-person or broker
- Provide a positive vibe. Value can be offered just by being pleasant to be around

- Offer support by sympathizing and/or empathizing
- Demonstrate kindness. Just be there for the other person

CHAPTER 57
A GREAT PRODUCT ISN'T ENOUGH: EXAMPLES OF TARGETING, POSITIONING, AND CHANNEL SELECTION DONE RIGHT

Building a great product isn't enough - you also need these 3 ingredients:

1. Right buyers
2. Right positioning
3. Right communication channels

RIGHT BUYERS

Does your product:

- Solve current
- Solve anticipated problems
- Create desired benefits

Lots of owners say they sell to "everyone". But "everyone" is not a market. Instead, pick specific, identifiable groups that your product can obviously help.

. . .

Examples:

- Fitness buffs who want to track workouts
- Freelance copywriters who need 1-click invoice creation
- High school students who need test prep for college entrance exams

RIGHT POSITIONING

Explain why YOU (rather than competitors) are uniquely suited to solving your buyer's specific problems or creating desired benefits.

Sell your strengths and downplay your weaknesses.

Your target buyers care most about certain specific things - not everything.

Examples:

- **Fast food:** Quick service & reasonable prices matter most to office workers on lunch break
- **Cleaning products:** Kid-safe, eco-friendly floor cleaners matter most to parents of young kids

RIGHT COMMUNICATION CHANNELS

Your buyers congregate on certain preferred platforms.

Meet them where they are:

- LinkedIn for B2B business owners
- Twitch for under-35 video gamers
- X/Twitter for SaaS copywriters

SUMMARY

A great product alone isn't enough. You also must:

- Sell to the right people
- Position yourself as uniquely suited for them compared to competing products
- Meet them at the places where they spend time and attention

CHAPTER 58
HERE ARE THE DIFFERENCES BETWEEN NICHING AND POSITIONING

Niching and positioning are often confused.

Here's how to quickly distinguish niching from positioning:

- **Niche** = A narrow slice of a specific market you sell to
- **Positioning** = How you communicate your differentiated capabilities to this narrow slice of the market

More specifically, niching is choosing a market and deciding on the problem you solve (or benefit you create) for buyers.

Positioning comes after selecting your niche.

It's the stance you stake out in communicating how you are the superior, differentiated solution to the other ways your users can create their desired outcomes.

CHAPTER 59
THREE MISTAKES THAT FIRST-TIME FOUNDERS COMMONLY MAKE WHEN BUILDING THEIR PRODUCT

These mistakes are unfortunately all too commonly made by 1st-time founders:

MISTAKE 1: THINKING JUST "WORKING HARD" IS ENOUGH, RATHER THAN DOING WHAT'S REQUIRED TO REALIZE AN OBJECTIVE

What's required may be beyond anything that's been demanded of you before.

Step up to what needs to be done, rather than what you think is enough. They're often very different.

MISTAKE 2: NOT LISTENING ENOUGH

Your customers have specific problems which require specific solutions.

Listen first and then talk, not the other way around.

MISTAKE 3: NOT ITERATING FAST ENOUGH

The idea you started out with may not be what the market wants.

Don't hold on for dear life - adapt and change!

CHAPTER 60
BUYERS DON'T ONLY JUDGE YOU BY YOUR PRICES

More than just prices, potential buyers are deciding whether or not your product can:

- Solve a current problem
- Solve an anticipated problem
- Create a desired benefit

Think about how you can fulfill one (or more) of these when creating your offer.

CHAPTER 61
WHAT'S THE BEST BALANCE BETWEEN WORK AND PERSONAL LIFE?

Some advocate for the maxim of "working to live and not living to work."

On the other end of the spectrum others champion a "hustle" work-focused lifestyle.

And others prescribe something between the two.

But you know what?

You choose what works for you at your current life stage, and where you want to go in the medium and long-term.

Are you just getting your business started and do you want (indeed, need) to put work as the primary focus of your life at the expense of your social and personal life?

Go ahead if that's the right choice for you.

Or maybe you've just become a first-time parent and you want to be there for your newborn by spending more time at home and down-shifting to a part-time role.

It's your decision.

Or maybe you're one to push aggressively with client work from Monday to Friday but then completely step away from emails and Slack messages on the weekend?

You do what works for you.

Just know that there will be interminable voices advocating for one position or another as you scroll through your different feeds.

But make sure you consciously choose what's right for YOU, your current life stage and future plans.

At the same time, you should ignore what doesn't work for you while accepting that YOUR choice may not be the right one for SOMEONE ELSE.

There's no "right" way to work and life - but there's certainly a wrong way to live it if it's incongruent with your objectives and goals.

CHAPTER 62
THE PURPOSE OF YOUR PRODUCT

Your product isn't primarily a piece of art or an expression of your deep emotional inner self.

Your product's primary purpose is to solve your buyer's problems and create desired benefits.

Make decisions not from emotion, but from logic.

Yet stir the emotions of your prospects and buyers.

CHAPTER 63
WHY FLEXIBILITY TRIUMPHS OVER PURE POWER IN EFFECTIVE COMMUNICATION

It's not always what you say (content) that counts, but how you communicate it.

And how you communicate something determines how strong your frame is.

THE PERSON WITH THE STRONGER FRAME WILL ALWAYS HAVE THE OVERALL UPPER HAND IN ANY INTERACTION

As you've probably experienced in your professional and personal life, the person with the stronger frame in any interaction almost always wins.

"Frame" could mean leveraging (but is not limited to):

- Greater physical presence (taller and/or brawnier)
- Louder (and/or shriller) voice
- Better articulating your perspective
- Having a more fully formed, nuanced internal point-of-view
- Various combinations of the above

As you can see, communication and the consequent frame it produces isn't always through verbal channels.

However, some of the strongest frames I've seen come from those who know their position, can elicit the other side's - and (if necessary) lean into the possibility of disagreement... even if conflict is something they normally shy away from in other areas of their life.

COMPARING THE POWER OF EFFECTIVE VS STRONG FRAMES

I've observed though, that the most effective frames (notice I said effective, not strongest) are often held by those who can do all of the above - yet they also have the flexibility to adjust their perspective when they encounter a different point-of-view.

By not being welded to any one particular point-of-view, these people can make more (and faster) progress in their professional and personal lives.

Why?

Because they can more frequently resolve (and move forward from) situations that otherwise turn into dead stops that sap forward momentum.

(Remember as a kid on the playground how much it hurt when you ran with pebbles in your shoes?)

Those who either run into roadblocks less frequently or can resolve them quicker can go on to take more meaningful actions (such as big projects) that allow them to accumulate wins on the scoreboard more quickly.

CHAPTER 64
'BUILD IT AND THEY WILL COME' IS THE WORST ADVICE FOR FOUNDERS

The biggest mistake founders make is building but not marketing.

Sometimes not marketing comes down to a lack of knowledge but sometimes it's operating under the mistaken belief that "a great product will sell itself".

Yes, in some cases a great (or good) product will go viral without much need for marketing spend.

The audio-chat app Clubhouse (remember them?) exploded in popularity due to exclusivity (it was invite-only) and the participation of high-profile celebrities and business leaders.

But they were an outlier and an exception to the rule.

To be honest, you are probably not an exception to the rule.

So if you're building a product (or have plans to), make sure you know how to create awareness in the market for what you're selling, and how to monetize that attention.

Otherwise you're just someone with a product, not a business.

CHAPTER 65
95% FAIL, 5% PREVAIL: CHARACTERISTICS THAT DEFINE THE MINORITY WHO WIN LONG-TERM

The best thing about going after any opportunities is that 95% of people put their head in the sand.

Because 95% of people fail to capitalize on life-enhancing opportunities, this means you're competing with 4 other people who've initially volunteered for the same opportunity.

Such opportunities can include Going-to-Market with a new SaaS product in a brand new space, publishing a book, starting a video channel or running a marathon.

The first person complains about being "so tired" all the time and never gets off the ground.

The second will have the daily energy but won't put in the work on a regular basis.

The third will have the consistency but not the skills for sustained success.

The fourth will have the skill and short-term consistency but will give up before critical mass is hit because their pain threshold is too low.

The fifth person will have the skill, consistency, energy, drive and sufficiently high pain threshold to succeed.

Only one actually makes it.

Will you be this fifth person - or one of the other four?

CHAPTER 66
SELL EFFECTIVELY BY FIRST CREATING THE EMOTIONAL STATES THAT GET PEOPLE TO TAKE THE ACTIONS THEY (AND YOU) WANT

"Effective selling is not about getting people to take the actions you want, but first creating the emotional states in them such that they want to take the actions you want."

Translation: First evoke the lizard brain emotions that underlie most of our actions rather than skipping that step and trying to compel action directly.

CHAPTER 67
THE UNSEEN ANCHOR: HOW DWELLING ON YESTERDAY'S SUCCESSES WILL DESTROY YOUR BUSINESS

One of the most dangerous things you can do as an entrepreneur is holding onto beliefs and practices that no longer serve you or your business.

MySpace. Kodak. Blockbuster. Blackberry.

These companies were once household names in their heydays, but all are shadows of their former dominant selves.

Often they're cited as cautionary tales of hanging too stubbornly onto obsolete ways of doing things.

Economics, technologies, laws and societies change with time.

As a result, customer preferences change.

When customer preferences change, so must the companies that serve them.

Those that fail to do so - whether knowingly or unknowingly - get "managed out" of the market.

There are 3 broad outcomes for companies when their environment changes to the extent that it renders existing business practices ineffective: adapt, stagnate or fail.

Which of these 3 buckets does your business fall into right now?

Is it stagnating?

Failing?

Or is it successfully adapting on an ongoing basis to consumer preferences that itself is making continual micro-adjustments in response to the changing macro environment?

If you're currently in the stagnating or failing bucket, which of the three do you ultimately want to end up in?

If you're not where you are right now, maybe you need to reconsider which of your beliefs and thoughts about yourself and the macro environment are actually serving you.

Next, find out what you need to transform those current beliefs and thoughts into.

Then, action your updated thoughts and beliefs in the physical world to effect real change instead of just thinking about it.

CHAPTER 68
ONE OF THE MOST POWERFUL LIFE SKILLS IS ADAPTABILITY

Adaptability has 2 parts:

1. Ability to adapt
2. Willingness to adapt

Those who:

- **Can't adapt** = tragic
- **Can adapt but refuse** = fools
- **Can and are willing** = gain the possibility (but not guarantee) of survival and ensuing success

Your only sure bet is if you:

> Can adapt + willing to adapt + willing to do the work

CHAPTER 69
HOW WELL ARE YOU NURTURING CUSTOMER RELATIONSHIPS BEYOND THE MAIN TRANSACTION? PROVIDING VALUE BEFORE, DURING, AND POST-TRANSACTION

How can you make your business stand out and ensure that it's seen as the first choice (or one of the first choices) in the market?

The key is to embed yourself at more touch points along the entire customer journey, and to provide your buyers relevant value at those touch points.

What this means in practice is providing value to your prospects and customers before, during and after the main transaction.

If you do this, you will enjoy increased Lifetime Value (LTV), retention and loyalty. You'll also have more repeat purchases by more deeply embedding buyers into your ecosystem.

Your goal is to provide value to your prospect or buyer that is relevant to their needs and desires at each of the 3 touch points so that you become their preferred choice (or THE preferred choice).

Here's how 3 companies in 3 different industries do this:

IKEA (HOME DECOR)

- **Before:** Online catalog, room inspiration and planning tools
- **During:** Huge selection of home furnishing products, in-store restaurants
- **After:** Assembly services, free replacement parts, generous return policy

MCDONALD'S (FAST FOOD)

- **Before:** App deals, Menu and nutrition information online
- **During:** Drive-thru service, McDelivery
- **After:** Customer feedback survey with incentives, loyalty rewards

SEPHORA (BEAUTY PRODUCTS)

- **Before:** Beauty Insider community for advice and trends
- **During:** Sales of cosmetics and other beauty items
- **After:** Beauty Insider rewards program

SUMMARY

To make your business the first choice in the market and stand out from competitors, provide value to prospects and customers throughout their entire journey - before, during, and after the main transaction.

Doing so builds loyalty, increases lifetime value, and makes you the preferred option.

CHAPTER 70
CUSTOMERS WANT AN OUTCOME, NOT ACTUALLY THE PRODUCT ITSELF

Customers buy your solution to achieve a desired end state, and not because they want your product or service itself.

What you're selling is merely a conduit for the achievement of a goal.

Five examples of what customers are actually buying

- **Customer buys from you:** Gym membership
- **What they actually want:** Improved health, weight loss or muscle gain

- **Customer buys from you:** Vacuum cleaner
- **What they actually want:** A clean home without time and effort of manual cleaning

- **Customer buys from you:** Meal kit membership
- **What they actually want:** Yummy home-cooked meals without having to go grocery shopping or recipe planning

- **Customer buys from you:** Tattoo
- **What they actually want:** Self-expression

- **Customer buys from you:** Health insurance policy
- **What they actually want:** Financial protection against unforeseen medical expenses

CHAPTER 71
BIG GAINS WITH MODEST EFFORT: THE POWER OF COMPOUNDED EXPONENTIAL GROWTH

One of the most important lessons I learned from marketing legend Jay Abraham is the concept of exponential growth.

Rather than trying to knock any one area out of the park, try instead to focus on smaller gains across a number of areas.

Let's say you shoot for a modest 10% improvement in three areas.

That's a 33% improvement in total.

That's a lot easier than trying to improve by 33% in one area alone.

It's a lot more difficult to raise a single area by a third, than to improve three separate areas by one-tenth each.

If you instead improve each area by 20%, then that's a compounded improvement of 73%.

These areas of improvement could be in any area of your life: business, finances, health, fitness, relationships, social life or any number of areas.

Try this when you're looking to achieve surprisingly big gains with modest effort.

And hey, this doesn't stop you from hitting home runs in the areas you want either.

CHAPTER 72
WHY YOUR "WIN" MIGHT NOT BE A WIN YET: AVOID PREMATURELY CELEBRATING UNTIL THE MONEY IS IN YOUR POCKET

Your experience does not automatically make reality.

What YOU think your prospect thinks, and what THEY actually think are two different things.

Just because you EXPERIENCED a good sales call doesn't mean your prospect came away convinced that your solution solved their problems (current or anticipated) or created a desired opportunity.

I've been in sales meetings where my colleagues high-fived immediately after the call, thinking they had closed the sale - only to be disappointed when the prospect came back with a no.

How you experienced an event isn't always commensurate with how the other party (or parties) in the interaction experienced that same event.

So until you actually have money in your pocket, save the celebrations for later.

CHAPTER 73
UNDERSTANDING CULTURAL NUANCES: THE UNDERESTIMATED SKILL IN MAKING INTERNATIONAL SALES

If you sell all over the world, how you "show up" to prospects and clients is a pretty significant contributor to the overall success of your meeting.

Often, success in sales and relationship management meetings has as much to do with how you communicate than just what you say.

The following has been my experience working in English-speaking, Western contexts and across Asia (Hong Kong, Mainland China, South Korea, Taiwan, Thailand, Malaysia and the rest of Southeast Asia).

Note: I speak as someone who has lived a big chunk of his life in Canada and a big chunk in Asia (primarily Hong Kong).

Here's a few observations from my time in Asia:

- **Names:** Use of honorifics such as Mr or Ms unless given permission to use their first name.
- **Body language:** Body language that is socially accepted in one part of the world may be considered overly emotive (and inappropriate in a professional setting) in another. I will usually use more restrained, controlled body language in Asia. If I am an "outsider" where I also don't speak the local

language (ie. when I visit South Korea or Thailand), I am even more conscious of not committing an unintentional social faux pas and will err even moreso on the side of conservative body language.

- **In-person meetings:** I will always accept business cards with both hands and then study it for a moment or two. When we are seated at the table, I never pocket the cards and instead place them face-up on the table for the duration of the meeting. For meetings with multiple people I go the additional step of arranging all cards side-by-side horizontally to sidestep any issues around "Richmond put my business card under another belonging to someone more junior than me"
- **Tonality:** Similar to body language, I'm very sensitive to who's who in the hierarchy and will adjust my tonality to match. A big danger is coming off as overly familiar, particularly to more senior clients and prospects. I make it a point to remind them through tonality that I'm the supplicant (not really true, but I knowingly play the part for the purposes of getting the sale or contract renewal).

CHAPTER 74
IS YOUR LACK OF OPTIONS UNDERMINING YOUR NEGOTIATING LEVERAGE?

If you stink at negotiation, here's one simple ironclad rule to improve your skills immediately:

"The power belongs to the person who can more so afford to walk away"

This one understanding will get you 90% of the way there in ALL your negotiations - whether it's with prospects, suppliers, employees or even in your personal life.

Sure, knowing specific, advanced negotiation strategies and tactics will absolutely help (go read *Getting More* by Stuart Diamond).

But just merely understanding that the highest leverage tool in your negotiation toolkit is "your greater ability to walk away from the deal than the person opposite you" will put you miles ahead of most negotiators.

For example, if you are even (say) 5% more willing to walk away than your counter-party, then you automatically have the upper hand in the negotiation.

And as you know, oftentimes, it's a lot more than just 5%.

So how do you increase your ability to walk away from deals you know are lukewarm (or even bad) - but which you don't have the current ability to turn down?

Simple - you increase your options.

INCREASE YOUR OPTIONS TO GET MORE NEGOTIATION LEVERAGE

By increasing your options I mean coming into your sales negotiation knowing you already have a bunch of warm, qualified leads sitting in your CRM so if this conversation doesn't pan out, you can just spin up other conversations.

It's walking into your lease renewal with your landlord knowing that you've already identified several other locations.

It's creating Standard Operating Procedures (SOPs) so that if one key employee leaves, you can easily bring their replacement up to speed (even better is if you cross-train existing employees to do some (or a substantial portion) of each others' jobs)

The more options you have, the less beholden to any one person, organization or circumstance turning out the way you want.

A big enterprise prospect tells you your product sucks and they'll never buy? No problem - you just go chat with someone else from your pipeline.

Your marketing manager (Pat) takes a hike?

Go ahead Pat.

You pull out your SOPs and plug-in another team member to tide things over until you hire a replacement.

Power and leverage in any negotiation starts with being able to walk away. And being able to walk away starts with creating - and then having - optionality.

Don't be afraid to use it.

What are you doing to build your optionality so that you can walk away from situations that don't benefit you the way you want?

CHAPTER 75
OUTGROWING PRODUCT OBSESSION: SUCCESS BEGINS WHEN YOU START MARKETING EVEN IF YOUR PRODUCT IS IMPERFECT

Stop acting only as a "product operator" and instead act like a business owner and start marketing.

In other words, are you like many new founders who overly focus on creating your product, yet fail to spend enough time and attention on marketing it?

I call this phenomenon Widget Obsession Syndrome.

WHAT ARE THE SYMPTOMS OF THIS SICKNESS?

Rather than the high fever, skin rashes and labored coughing of other diseases, symptoms of Widget Obsession Syndrome include:

- An overly myopic obsession with "getting your product 'perfectly perfect'"
- Failing to do enough (and the right type) of marketing that's right for your target market because you spend all your time and energy on perfecting or over-engineering your widget
- Ignoring other critical parts of your business that could be

bigger growth bottlenecks (poor positioning, ineffective sales processes, etc)

The fallout of Widget Obsession Syndrome includes lackluster conversions, stunted sales, poor retention and a very frustrated (and stressed) you.

As a coach and consultant to new founders launching their first products, I regularly talk to plenty of Widget Obsession Syndrome victims.

WHAT'S THE CURE?

Simple - stop acting only as a "product operator".

Instead spend more time as an actual BUSINESS OWNER managing your overall business machinery (your highest and best use).

What this means in real-world practical action is:

- **Cure #1:** A strong consistent focus on marketing and sales. Additional incremental improvements to your product aren't going to fill your funnel with qualified leads and convert those leads into users / customers. Only marketing & sales does.
- **Cure #2:** Get your product (ie. your widget) to a point that's good enough or above average (but it doesn't need to be "perfect")
- **Cure #3:** Look at the entirety of your business. Look for bottlenecks OUTSIDE product development. Reasons could be ineffective marketing copy, confusing UX, bad customer service...or maybe you've picked target markets completely wrong by trying to sell (for example) life insurance to the dead. Obviously that particular market doesn't want or need that.

WHY DO THESE WORK?

A perfect 100-point product multiplied by zero sales and marketing will always be a big fat zero.

However, an 80-point product multiplied by great 90-point marketing and sales totals 7200 pts.

As famed management consultant & author (of 35+ books) Peter Drucker said *"Because the purpose of business is to create a customer, the business enterprise has two - and only two - basic functions: marketing and innovation."*

Too many founders overly obsess on product to the detriment of marketing - and consequently damage their whole business in real, measurable, painful ways.

You could have the greatest most perfectly perfect product in the world but if no one knows you're selling it (or you're selling to the wrong people) then nothing matters.

In short, get your product into a good enough (or above average) state and hit your marketing and sales hard.

Then you'll actually begin to see the gains you expected when you started this journey as a founder AND business owner.

CHAPTER 76
THIS FACTOR IS HARDER THAN BUILDING A GREAT PRODUCT

Building a great product isn't the hardest part of business.

Instead, it's building, keeping and growing your audience because they're bombarded daily with promises of faster, cheaper, better or different ways of doing things.

You're relevant to buyers only if you work to stay so.

CHAPTER 77
HOW TO CAPTURE PRODUCT-MARKET FIT BY TWEAKING YOUR PRODUCT, OFFER, AND PRICE

Here's how getting Product, Offer and Price (POP) right at the same time get you closer to Product-Market-Fit (PMF).

PRODUCT

Does your widget do one (or more things) to solve a problem and/or create new desired opportunities for your potential buyer?

"Solving a problem" means either a current or anticipated problem.

"Create new desired opportunities" means creating new possibilities that would not have otherwise been possible without use of your product - and which are also WANTED by your prospect.

- **Want** = Strawberry ice cream and Snickers bars (yay!)
- **Need** = Oatmeal and raw broccoli (for health)

Why the distinction?

Because many purchases have a strong emotional component so make sure you learn how to elicit, arouse and intensify wants.

Luxury watches costing 4 to 5 figures (or higher) such as Rolex, Patek

Philippe, A. Lange & Sohne are all examples of purchases driven primarily by emotion.

Breakthrough Advertising by Eugene Schwartz has a good rundown of how to elicit, arouse and intensify Wants

OFFER

Sweeten your offer to give people compelling reasons to give you their money.

Be careful to differentiate your offer from your product.

Let's take a simple example:

- **Product** = Samsung 25.1 cu. ft. 3-door french door refrigerator in stainless steel
- **Offer** = 15 day no questions asked returns + free installation and disposal of your old fridge + free shipping + 1 year extended warranty + the dang fridge

As you can see, you can sweeten the appeal of doing business with you by adding in additional non-product services or products to stand out amongst (1.) direct competition and (2.) adjacent alternatives that solve the same problem as you.

An example of an adjacent alternative is when people buy Arm & Hammer baking soda not as a leavening agent for food preparation (its original use), but as an inexpensive, effective deodorizer.

PRICE

People are more likely to give you money when they are (from their perspective) getting more perceived value out of your product than what they are paying.

So for example, they get 100 units of value (in the form of something that solves a problem and/or improves their life) while giving up 60 units of value (in the form of money)

If you play around at the same time with the above 3 levers of POP (Product, Offer and Price), you will be able to attract paying users.

THE FINAL STEP

Getting POP right isn't enough.

You must also effectively COMMUNICATE through the appropriate channels (eg. Youtube, X/Twitter, Instagram, etc) to a RECEPTIVE DEMOGRAPHIC using proper POSITIONING.

Now go get PMF'ed.

CHAPTER 78
FOUR WAYS TO INVITE UNEXPECTED NEW OPPORTUNITIES

Get more opportunities by focusing on developing:

- Monetizable skills
- Openness to serendipity
- Relationships with teachers AND their gatekeepers
- A focus on moving with (not against) technological trends

You can't plan 100% of life, but you can shape it.

CHAPTER 79
DISCOUNT TODAY, PROFIT TOMORROW: THE POWER OF FRONT-LOADING VALUE OVER PUSHING FOR IMMEDIATE FULL GAIN

Here's what 50% discounted pizza will teach new founders about maximizing Lifetime Value and referrals - and put more cash in your pocket.

A new Domino's pizza joint opened up near my house the other day offering half off on all pizzas as a "grand opening" offer.

Having had Domino's before, I was a bit skeptical about the quality, but hey - half off is half off, right?

So I bit the bullet.

So imagine my surprise when, unlike my last experience with another Domino's location 3 years ago, the pizza this time was GOOD.

Very good in fact

Lots of fresh, thick-cut meat and veggie pieces *generously* arrayed over a moistly supple base baked to perfection. We're talking chunky Italian sausage, ham, champignon button mushrooms, red onions, extra cheese - the whole works.

And none of that excessive greasiness from before. Wonderful.

More importantly, they gave away probably 1.5x - 2x the volume of ingredients other stores would use on their pies.

And this Domino's spot was probably doing this for ALL the other pizzas they sold.

HOW DOES DISCOUNTED PIZZA APPLY TO MAXIMIZING LTV AND REFERRALS?

Simple - they created new repeat buyers and word-of-mouth

I'm definitely going back even if they (understandably) cut back on the amount of ingredients they use and even when they get rid of the 50% discount at some point.

Others are likely thinking exactly like me too.

This store knew their margins and how much could be "given away" to acquire each new buyer

Don't just think about maximizing short-term profitability at the expense of medium and longer-term profitability.

This Domino's joint deliberately temporarily cut into their short-term margin to create new repeat customers and referrals.

The lesson from this story is that when deciding on pricing and your offer, be willing to "leave some money on the table".

You don't need to "capture all the value" in the first transaction.

MOST OF BUSINESS ISN'T A BINARY CASE OF WIN-LOSE

Rather, it's about creating situations where you perhaps may lose a bit on the initial sale, but win big on LTV via repeat purchases of the same products, up-sells to higher priced items and cross-sells on other horizontals produced in-house or in partnership with another company.

You also win when customers drive referrals, thus lowering your overall Customer Acquisition Cost (CAC).

Businesses don't win by winning once. They win by consistently winning on a consistent basis and knowing their financial picture.

SUMMARY

Knowing your margins will allow you to play the long game.

This includes strategically leaving some money on the table to provide drastically more value to your buyers than what they paid. Then watch your referrals and LTV skyrocket to put more cash in your pocket.

CHAPTER 80
GUIDE PROSPECTS TO A DECISION THEY'RE INVESTED IN MAKING RATHER THAN PRESSURING THEM

Which sales strategy is better?

- **Option 1:** Overtly pushing prospects to buy via pressure, pestering and pleading
- **Option 2:** Covertly guiding prospects to experience emotions that LEAD them to buy because THEY believe it benefits them

CHAPTER 81
CONTINUALLY DOMINATE NARROW NICHES TO GROW YOUR STARTUP

Here's the best, most tried-and-true way to grow your startup into the muscular Big Company you dreamed about when you started this journey.

Start by finding a NARROW niche that you can serve by either solving a problem and/or creating an opportunity.

Dominate that niche and then leverage your cash flow, credibility (eg. reference users and testimonials), word-of-mouth and marketing (paid and non-paid) to expand into an adjacent niche.

Rinse and repeat over and over until you have a big company.

Most new founders try to target a market that's way too broad (i.e. "We serve everybody").

No.

You'll never get traction that way because you'll have to dislodge an entrenched, incumbent MegaCorp with way more firepower than you.

What you instead want is a narrow niche that you can DOMINATE.

Dominate a narrow niche.

Expand into a new adjacent niche.

Dominate that new narrow niche.

Expand into another new adjacent niche

Dominate that new narrow niche.

It's that simple.

SUMMARY

- **Step 1:** Focus on a specific market niche. Don't bite off more than you can chew with a broad market - that's for giant MegaCorps with more money and resources than you have

- **Step 2:** Dominate your specific niche by consistently hammering these 3 levers:

- Consistent marketing
- A high-quality product / service. Do not confuse this with "perfect"
- Memorable end-to-end customer service (to ensure repeat business)

- **Step 3:** Expand into a new adjacent market you can credibly compete in and get Product-Market-Fit using the same three levers in Step 2

- **Step 4:** Repeat over and over until your fledging SaaS startup is the Big Company you envisioned all along

CHAPTER 82
PERFECTION WILL KILL YOU: LAUNCHING AT 80% IS GOOD ENOUGH FOR MOST OF YOU

One mistake I've consistently seen new founders make is waiting too long to launch.

This includes new features, products and marketing campaigns.

For most of you, 80% is good enough - you don't need perfection.

An 80% effort will be enough to start making money, getting users, gathering feedback and whatnot.

It's more important to release with a very capable 80% effort than delay indefinitely until a 100% Rolls-Royce deliverable is achieved.

Of course, there are certain industries where you can't get away with 80% effort: I'm thinking fintech, law and medical. In such spaces, you definitely want to cross all your t's and cross all your i's.

But for everyone else, speed of execution and learning are essential.

You think these chapters I write are perfect?

Of course not. But they're good enough to publish while allowing me sufficient time and energy to write my other books, post on my socials and create products to grow my audience.

For most people, you should prioritize speed and learning over getting things perfectly perfect.

Because if you're a perfectionist at heart (like me), you'll spend forever trying to touch up tiny imperfections your market won't even notice at the very real expense of making material progress in your business.

And you definitely wouldn't want to win your many little battles but lose the war.

CHAPTER 83
LIKES DON'T EQUAL PRODUCT-MARKET FIT: REVENUE IS THE REAL INDICATOR

Stop lying to yourself by thinking likes and kudos mean you have Product-Market-Fit (PMF).

Likes (whether online or offline) by themselves only indicate you are getting CLOSER to achieving PMF.

Instead, look for the money.

If you're making *some* money, then you have *some* PMF.

The key thing to keep in mind is that the more, faster and easier you're making that money, the stronger your PMF.

Just remember not to confuse *approaching* PMF with actually getting *some initial* PMF.

CHAPTER 84
HOW TO PINPOINT YOUR BEST CUSTOMERS WITH THE 3-STEP FRAMEWORK OF RECENCY, FREQUENCY, AND MONETARY VALUE

Here's how to find your highest leverage customer segments in 3 steps.

Use the RFM Model to segment and prioritize your highest value and highest potential customer groups.

RFM stands for Recency, Frequency and Monetary Value.

The more recently, frequently and the higher the monetary value assigned to a customer, the more valuable they are.

Here's a more granular breakdown:

DID THEY BUY MORE RECENTLY?

These customers generally have a higher probability of making a repeat purchase in the *near future*.

No guarantees they will solidify into CONSISTENT buyers though.

DID THEY BUY MORE FREQUENTLY?

This is a measure of loyalty.

You can count on these customers to buy more CONSISTENTLY over time for the duration of their relationship with you.

But it's not indicative that they will buy soon.

Maybe they'll buy 6 weeks from now - or 6 months...or 6 years.

But you can count on them to keep buying (at least moreso than the other two categories).

DID THEY BUY MORE IN TERMS OF MONETARY VALUE?

Those who buy your big ticket offers are more likely to buy another high-priced product. These are your "whales".

SUMMARY

The RFM model is a simple way to ensure you:

- Focus your limited time and resources
- Appropriately target your offers to the right parts of your customer list

CHAPTER 85
THE ONLY 3 WAYS TO INCREASE REVENUE

Your levers are:

1. **Increase the number of customers:** Turn more people into buyers
2. **Increase purchase frequency:** Get people buying more often from you
3. **Increase average transaction size:** Get each person to accumulate more total spending

CHAPTER 86
90% OF PRODUCT-MARKET FIT IS REALLY JUST THESE 3 FACTORS

The three factors are:

- Targeting the right audience
- Putting an offer that solves an urgent and important pain for them
- Using words, images, video and audio that shows them how their life could change by buying your offer

Simple in concept.

But much more difficult to nail in the real world.

CHAPTER 87
HOW TO DO LEAD GEN WITH ZERO AD BUDGET: THE POWER OF PARTNERSHIPS

No budget for paid ads as a new founder?

No problem.

While social media, SEO, cold DMs and emails are all effective means of lead generation, you're most likely overlooking one of the cheapest lead generation methods that (assuming you targeted the proper markets to begin with) *also* has some of the highest conversion rates.

What exactly is this wonderful low-cost, high impact method?

Partnerships - ie. borrowing credibility.

In other words, taking someone else's light and shining it on yourself.

WHY USE PARTNERSHIPS TO GENERATE LEADS?

In the same way that having Google, Amazon, Goldman Sachs or McKinsey on your CV confers a halo effect on a jobseeker, borrowing credibility as a startup means taking on the goodwill of another entity that has accumulated more goodwill, more trust or more reputation than you have right now.

For a software dev tools company I worked with, this meant partnering with a well-known industry conference to give exclusive complimentary access to my client's product.

Qualified leads would be onboarded onto the software and an upsell would be made several weeks later once users had been acquainted with the platform.

For the conference organizer, this meant they could sweeten the attendee goodie bag and thus provide an additional incentive to help push would-be attendees into buying a ticket.

For my client it meant a low-cost way to generate qualified leads in reasonable volume with a minimum of ongoing work because he intelligently leveraged the reputation and credibility of the conference organizer.

End result: a win-win for both parties.

FINDING PARTNERSHIPS REQUIRES REACHING OUT TO PEOPLE

By the way, notice I said that partnerships are one of the CHEAPEST ways of generating leads.

I DIDN'T say it's one of the "easiest" - and that's because if you don't already have a warm contact to hit up, it requires that you go out and find qualified partners by doing Big Scary Cold Outreach.

But you know what? That just means plenty more for you if you're willing to take a tiny step outside your comfort zone because other new founders will be too scared to pluck what is essentially lower-hanging fruit.

Will you go out to harvest these easier pickings for a low-cost high leverage result by stepping outside your known knowns into the known unknowns and unknown unknowns?

The decision is entirely up to you.

But it's almost certain that you and your business will end up for the better for it if you can handle this upfront bit of social pressure.

CHAPTER 88
WILL YOUR BEHAVIOR HELP OR HURT YOU? THE ROLE OF COURTESY IN THE SMALL WORLD OF INDUSTRY RELATIONSHIPS

Showing courtesy to people goes a long way because you never know how the tables will flip down the line.

The guy you ghosted might be the one in a position to say yes or no to your job candidacy a few years from now.

At the very least, you might end up working in the same (or adjacent) departments.

And in certain industries (eg. tech, law, banking, consulting) or cities (eg. Hong Kong, where I spent a good chunk of my career) where everyone knows everyone else, it pays extra to be courteous as you never know how the tables will flip.

Surprises do happen.

It's also a (very) small world.

I remember several years ago in the check-in line at Incheon airport (near Seoul) when within the span of 15 minutes I bumped into two guys I knew.

One was someone whose wife had invited us to dinner at their place in Hong Kong the week before and another was someone I had met about 6 months before in Singapore.

And all 3 of us in Korea on that same November afternoon transiting to different parts of the world from the same airport.

Again, it's a small world.

CHAPTER 89
HOW YOUR COMPETITION'S MARKETING MIGHT BE BEATING YOUR FAR SUPERIOR PRODUCT

Not getting the traction you want?

It may be the case that your competition is marketing better than you, and not that your product is objectively worse than theirs.

"Marketing better" could mean they are more precisely identifying target segments, using the right channels (offline/online) or communicating using the right messaging once the right segments and right channels have been found.

It could even mean that they're marketing more than you in terms of volume – ie. impressions, optimizing for click-throughs and converting on the Call-to-Actions.

And it could be all of the above – or more.

This idea also applies to other areas of life, including careers and your personal brand.

In what parts of your life and/or business are you underserving yourself by not creating enough awareness?

CHAPTER 90
STOP HEDGING: MAKE CLEAN CUT DECISIONS TO MOVE FASTER

Sometimes the easiest way to clear your mental clutter is just to make "clean cut" decisions.

By clean cut, I mean a definitive choice - it's either a clear yes or a clear no.

No hedging bets or equivocation - just a crystal-clear choice that leads to real action in the physical world.

Will they always be ideal decisions where the pros definitively and decisively outweigh the cons?

Probably not.

But what's far more important is that you've cleared out the mental bramble that's actively preventing or considerably impeding significant progress in your business and personal life.

CHAPTER 91
PEOPLE USE LOGIC TO JUSTIFY EMOTIONAL WANTS

"Macs make me more creative"
"Nike shoes make me a better athlete"
"Moleskine notebooks make me more organized"

None of the above are true.

But it shows that people regularly use logic to justify emotion-driven purchases.

Just something to remember.

CHAPTER 92
HOW CONFIDENCE AND OUTCOME INDEPENDENCE WILL MOVE YOU FORWARD

Pairing confidence with outcome independence will move mountains in your business and personal life.

How?

- **Confidence** = Belief in yourself, abilities and worth
- **Outcome Independence** = Emotionally detached from any one way of doing things
- **Confidence + Outcome Independence** = You trust in your ability to navigate new opportunities while staying open to unexpected possibilities

In other words, you believe in your ability to take on new challenges while freeing yourself from the idea that there's only one "right" way to do it

Put another way:

With confidence, you don't shy away from fears or anxiety. You know it's there - but you keep going.

With outcome independence, you can pivot fluidly to discover (or invent) new ways to achieve your goals.

Put both together and you give yourself the "yes" attitude and flexibility to keep aggressively iterating until you get to where you want.

CHAPTER 93
YOUR PRODUCT IS NOT YOUR OFFER

The difference between your product and your offer:

- **Product** = the widget
- **Offer** = the widget + price + all else your buyer gets

A practical example:

- **Product** = Fridge (Samsung w/ french doors, 24 cu ft)
- **Offer** = $1700 for the fridge + 3 year warranty + free delivery + home installation

CHAPTER 94
IT'S A MISTAKE TO ONLY FOCUS ON THE INITIAL SALE

Rather than only focusing short-term on the first sale, you should instead think from the beginning about how you will successfully sell the renewal.

Why?

Because it puts you in an ongoing mindset of maximizing Lifetime Value (LTV).

This forces you to continually:

- Deliver continual or new value in your core product that is relevant and important
- Destroy the "one and done" mentality of one-time sales
- Expand your portfolio of product cross-sells

DELIVERING CONTINUAL OR NEW VALUE IN YOUR CORE PRODUCT THAT IS RELEVANT AND IMPORTANT

Customers renew subscriptions when you deliver ongoing or new value that is both:

- Relevant (they care about it)

- Important (has consequential bearing on their life)

Examples:

- **Relevant + Important** = Pain in their left chest (could be a heart attack)
- **Relevant + Unimportant** = Deciding which movie to watch on a Friday night
- **Irrelevant + Important** = For most people in their early 20s, retirement planning (it's important but most people in this age bracket don't care)
- **Irrelevant + Unimportant** = Blue or black ink to sign a document

Knowing that subscription renewals come from solving relevant and important problems focuses you on building features that actually matter to your buyers.

DESTROY THE "ONE AND DONE" MENTALITY OF ONE-TIME SALES:

People generally buy from people they like – or at least respect.

Prioritizing renewal success from the very first sale incentivizes you to treat your customer relationship with a long-term view – specifically one that encourages you to take the actions necessary to ensure your buyer sees you as their ongoing preferred choice over potential alternatives.

This could mean:

- Exclusive access to beta product releases or early releases
- Proactive account monitoring and issue resolution
- Regular check-ins calls and meetings

While "liking" is not a necessary prerequisite for ongoing commercial relationships (I'm sure you've bought from people or companies you didn't care for), it's an easy way to bolster your renewal rates.

EXPAND YOUR CROSS-SELL PORTFOLIO

You can only squeeze so much revenue from renewals of your core product - or even upsells to more advanced versions of it.

Focusing on successful renewal sales forces you to continuously develop your product portfolio with cross-sells that complement your core product.

Examples:

- iPhone + AirPods
- Samsung Smart TV + Samsung Sound Bar
- Nike shoes + Nike running apparel
- Lego building set + Lego mini-figures

In other words, what could you sell that would enhance the experience of using your core product?

SUMMARY

Focusing on successfully selling the renewal incentives you to meaningfully:

- Shift focus from the initial sale to producing successful renewals that maximize LTV
- Deliver continual and new value in your core product that is both relevant and important to buyers
- Destroy the "one and done" mentality of one-time sales and force you to take concrete actions that keep you in buyers' good graces so that you remain their preferred choice
- Force you to expand your cross-sell portfolio to continually expand your LTV

CHAPTER 95
OVERWORKED? SEVEN SIMPLE WAYS TO WIN BACK MORE TIME

Win back more time by implementing at least one of these ways into your workflow:

DELEGATE

Give the work to someone else on your team.

This will be for tasks that still need to get done, but which are not the highest and best use of your time, skills and/or talents.

OUTSOURCE

Hire someone outside your company to do this.

This could be because no one inside your company (including you) has this skill.

For example, maybe you've decided to create YouTube videos as part of your updated marketing strategy but you don't want to take the time to learn video production yourself nor to spend time and/or money training someone on your team. Therefore, you hire an outside agency to take care of it.

ELIMINATE

Just stop doing it - forever.

CONSOLIDATE

Combine multiple tasks into one.

Often very effective when you combine several tasks from the same (or similar) category.

For example, you may designate a "Meeting Day" and consolidate all your meetings (normally spread throughout the week) into that day.

DOWNSIZE

Streamline the number of steps or moving parts.

DEFER

Push off these tasks until a pre-determined date or indefinitely. This is different from eliminating it because you plan to get back to it at some point.

AUTOMATE

Find a way to put one of your routines on autopilot. This could include using appointment scheduling tools (eg. Calendly), automated testing for software development and lead scoring features in CRM platforms.

SUMMARY

The 7 ways to reclaim your time are:

1. Delegate
2. Outsource
3. Eliminate

4. Consolidate
5. Downsize
6. Defer
7. Automate

CHAPTER 96
BIG SOCIAL MEDIA CREATORS ARE USEFUL TO LEARN FROM, BUT ONLY IF YOU KNOW WHAT TO FOCUS ON AND WHAT TO IGNORE

Beware of those who speak predominately in absolutist statements ("always", "must", "will", etc).

In fact there are a few big creators on LinkedIn and X/Twitter who do this quite often - either because they believe it, or because they know it gets eyeballs (or a combination of both).

I won't name names but you've likely read their stuff.

Heck, I even bought social media growth courses from some of them.

But my suggestion is to focus mainly on analyzing how they grew such large, engaged audiences on different social platforms rather than to also blindly follow the life or business advice they give in their posts.

There's often some correlation with follower count and the quality of that writer's life / business advice (otherwise it wouldn't be positively validated by so many people) but taking all their advice at face value all the time is dangerous.

But this is just my perspective.

CHAPTER 97
FIVE LIFE-CHANGING HABITS FOR YOUR BUSINESS AND PERSONAL LIFE

1. Be at peace with devoting a season of your life to work
2. Read outside your normal areas of interest
3. Be the first person to introduce yourself
4. Cold-emailing, cold-DMing, cold-calling
5. Building relationships before you need them

CHAPTER 98
ARE WE ABANDONING ACCOUNTABILITY FOR A FEELINGS-FOCUSED WORK CULTURE?

A big problem with much leadership thinking these days is it's fashionable to focus excessively around feelings and feeling good.

What's missing is accountability to oneself, one's team and one's clients.

Before you come at me with pitchforks and burning torches - let me explain.

COMPANIES MUST PRODUCE VALUE TO SURVIVE

In order to exist (and continue to exist), most organizations need to produce something of value (either a physical product and/or intangible service).

These outputs must be created on a timeline and at a quality-level that buyers will accept to the extent that they will open their wallets and hand over money (or some other form of payment).

The only way these outputs can be made and delivered to such standards is consistent *commitment* on the vendor side to meeting these standards.

Now, humans being humans, we do (and will) slip up from time to time.

The only way to uphold such commitments to customers (and continue to get paid by them) is a vendor-side system of identifying, declaring and fixing extant slippages and impediments to said commitments.

And that's where accountability comes in - i.e. to clean up one's slippages so as to meet stated commitments.

ACCOUNTABILITY DOESN'T CARE IF YOU "DON'T FEEL GOOD" OR IF YOU'RE "JUST NOT IN THE MOOD TODAY".

Accountability is saying "You know what? I forgot to send you the churn analysis spreadsheet last Tuesday, but I own up to it and I commit to getting it to you by tomorrow evening."

It's "I've got the flu, so I'm letting you know that I won't be able to work at my best today. I propose to take the rest of today (Monday) and tomorrow (Tuesday) off to recover. By Wednesday I will have recovered and I commit to sending you the marketing copy for our landing page redesign."

In other words, take ownership of the slippage, commit to a solution ALONG with a new timeframe and then ACTUALLY deliver on that solution in the promised timeframe.

It's as simple as that - and it doesn't need to conflict with a pleasant working environment. Or feeling good about oneself and making others feel good.

But I've found that prioritizing "feeling good" as the #1 priority over accountability tends to introduce the possibility of using bad feelings (basically tiny squirts of chemicals in our brains) to avoid delivering on time (and with quality) work we find difficult, or are nervous about

WHERE DOES THIS LEAVE YOU AS A FOUNDER?

Big companies can afford commitment and accountability slippages because they often have large cash cushions, big marketing budgets, and established product lines to paper over deficiencies.

But as a new founder you often don't have any of those advantages - heck, you may not even yet have a *single* product that's ready to sell.

So you better get working, fixing and delivering *in spite* of your feelings.

CHAPTER 99
LIVING IN PAST GLORY: IS IT TIME TO UPDATE YOUR PERSONAL NARRATIVE?

There is a half-life to all your accomplishments.

There will be a point where the luster of being ex-Google, ex-Meta or ex-McKinsey fades.

Of course, the positive afterglow and halo effect of having a big brand name on your CV is very real.

Why do you think so many ex-McKinsey, BCG or Bain consultants end up in the C-suite of so many major companies?

But if you haven't done so, at some point you need to start building your success in the present (and into the future) - instead of relying on your past successes.

Your badge of honor as an ex-Google employee might still be fresh at 9 months out, but it starts becoming a problem if 9 years later your primary professional success is still "ex-Google guy".

You'll notice that I put ex-Reuters in my LinkedIn headline.

That's a deliberate marketing move on my part because I know Reuters is a fairly well known and respected international brand name.

But my last day with that company was a long time ago.

So while I put "ex-Reuters" in my headline and in my outreach, I do so primarily to catch the attention of my audience and prospects. In other words, you never get the chance to talk to someone if you can't even catch their attention in the first place.

But I've learned and grown a lot professionally since I left that job in 2016.

So while it's useful to have that international brand on my CV, I make sure to continually update my skills and meet new people to ensure I'm still relevant in today's marketplace, as well as going forward.

So...make sure you're not living off past glory and past professional pedigree.

There is a half-life to your professional accomplishments and it's ticking away.

Go create something new.

ABOUT THE AUTHOR

Richmond Wong, a Toronto native, works directly with founders and senior decision makers of early-stage startups to take them from zero to launch and growth.

At the time of this writing, he's helped 150+ startups around the world with their highest ROI growth, product and launch initiatives.

He previously launched enterprise B2B software for Reuters and Lexis-Nexis in 10+ international markets including Korea, Singapore, Hong Kong, Taiwan, Malaysia and throughout Southeast Asia.

As a result of these varied international experiences, his approach combines the agility of nimble startup methodologies with the rigor of real-world tested enterprise-grade processes.

Before moving into software, he trained as a corporate lawyer with one of the world's ten largest law firms, Hogan Lovells, serving Fortune 500 clients on their most mission critical mandates.

Richmond started his career as a journalist with Rogers Publishing, part of one of Canada's largest media companies.

Visit www.richmondwong.com for his latest writings, books and products.

Made in the USA
Las Vegas, NV
18 April 2025

21091336R00118